the simple path of holiness

BOOK 1

For Those with Unanswered Questions & Difficult Life Conditions

By Will Raymond

Published by:

Sacred Books Publishing Company.

www.sacredbooks.com

The Simple Path of Holiness

Original copyright 2004 Will Raymond

First edition @ copyright Will Raymond 2012

Published by the Sacred Books Publishing Company*

P.O. Box 1725, Clinton, MA 01510

978-761-1213

www.sacredbooks.com

info@sacredbooks.com

ISBN 978-0-578-08772-6

*Sacred Books Publishing Company is a DBA of
Raymond Business Services LLC
P.O. 1725, Clinton, MA 01510

Dedication

For all who are not sure what to believe.

For all who struggle to find the healing and relief they seek.

For all who were ostracized, imprisoned, tortured, or killed for their efforts to practice and express their religious and spiritual beliefs, and those who now live under present threat.

For all who lived in fear, in ages past, of negative priestly, ministerial, or clerical castes and those now living who have similar fears.

Permissions Acknowledgements

The author wishes to acknowledge and thank the following for permissions to use excerpts from the following texts.

Page 23 Originally from *Spiritual Autobiography of Charles de Foucauld*, ed. Jean Francois Six, trans. H. Holland Smith (New York: P.J. Kennedy & Sons, 1964).

Page 26 First Reference- From *The Collected Works of St. John of the Cross*, translated by Kieran Kavanaugh and Otilio Rodriguez. Copyright © 1964, 1979, 1991 by Washington Province of Discalced Carmelites. ICS Publications, 2131 Lincoln Road, N.E. Washington, DC 20002-1199, www.icspublications.org.

Page 26 Second Reference- From *The Hidden Life*, by Edith Stein. Copyright © 1992 Washington Province of Discalced Carmelites. ICS Publications, 2131 Lincoln Road, N.E. Washington, DC 20002-1199 www. icspublications.org.

Page 177 and Page 250 From *Practicing the Jhānas*, by Stephen Snyder & Tina Rasmussen. © 2009 by Stephen Snyder and Tina Rasmussen. Reprinted by arrangement with Shambhala Publications Inc., Boston, MA, www.shambhala.com.

Contents

Prelude

1.

Some people have a particularly strong need to know the highest truths of this life and the most effective ways to diminish suffering in the world. Unfortunately, quite a few who are driven by these elemental needs encounter a general problem in their search when they turn to the various religions of the world. They find they either do not understand or cannot accept many of the traditional answers provided by different religions to their most important questions. Whether they are studying ancient or very modern faith traditions, many find that much of what they read or hear about is unbelievably confusing or just plain mistaken. It is not that such people fail to see the value, irreplaceable beauty, and truth that are also very real aspects of various religious faiths. The problem is they find many teachings of religion not only do not help them, but the errors and violent dysfunction they encounter only make things worse. An even more serious set of doubts arise when they come to realize that the atavistic rigidity and gross hypocrisy of many deeply religious people are primary causes of the suffering in the larger society in which they live.

For others their needs are more simply stated.

Despite their best efforts with religion, psychology, or meditation they have not found an effective way to resolve the painful hardships of their life or to find relief from difficult emotional states. They continue to hope a more clear understanding of truth will help them cultivate the exalted experiences of peace and deep healing they have heard are possible. Part of the general challenge for many in this predicament is they cannot find any clear way to sort out the important truths from the distorting errors they encounter in a particular culture they are drawn to.

For anyone who experiences these kinds of painful frustration, it is dearly hoped this independent commentary on silent meditation will be of real help.

2.

Those people who have chosen a particular faith tradition and feel they do generally accept the teachings of their tradition can also find benefit from these practices.

This is because everyone who makes a serious study of spirituality or philosophy experiences times when they really are not certain how to understand the more perplexing teachings of their tradition. This is especially true when people experience sudden and devastating loss, or violent attack, betrayal or heartbreak in love, or raw injustice. Even the most committed life-long believers can find their faith is shaken to the core during such difficult times. It is to help people, regardless of their present levels of faith or confusion, with both the small trials of life and those that push people to the limits of their endurance, that the practices of the simple path are offered.

It is not the intent of this commentary to attempt to persuade people to accept or reject particular beliefs or points of view. Rather the primary purpose of this commentary on silent meditation is to offer general but very effective practices that people can adapt to their present beliefs and life experience as they search for a way forward that feels true to them.

3.

For both those who have made strong commitments to particular beliefs and those who are quite unsure about what to believe, there is a general theme that will help them find the way forward.

When you encounter a question you cannot answer, or an answer to a serious question that makes no sense to you, it is important to set those questions and answers aside, at least for the time being.

You can return to them at a later time if and when you feel it makes sense to do so.

It is enough to think carefully about the positive teachings and values you do understand and are freely willing to accept. It is enough to be very honest about where you know you could be making better efforts with your core beliefs, however general and basic those core beliefs may be.

It is enough to search for ways to make those better efforts, at a realistic pace, over time.

This is the simple path.

4.

Very sincere and consistent efforts with those teachings and values you do understand and can freely accept will generate at least early stages of peace and clarity. The lessons learned from these efforts and early stages of peace and clarity will help you see better ways to resolve painful situations. These lessons will help you further simplify your life and perspectives in ways that will make deeper practice and insight possible.

All of this will help calm and clear your mind by degrees.

As the mind clears, consciousness will be refined.

As consciousness is refined, you will always be able to sense a good general direction forward to whatever is the next level of peace and understanding that is available to you.

As you are able to progress to significantly deeper experiences of peace and clarity your faculties of consciousness and perception will become noticeably enhanced. These enhancements to consciousness will allow you to return to any unanswered questions you set aside earlier, which you still find to be relevant, with far greater levels of skill. Upon additional careful reflection you may be able to gain the insight needed to resolve unanswered questions, or you may realize they never really were quite the right questions to begin with. In either eventuality your mind will be lighter and clearer and you will be more free.

What is important is to have a basic faith and curiosity that increasingly sophisticated levels of peace and understanding are available to you, even if the evidence of your life to date would seem to dramatically contradict this point.

With each new threshold of peace and clarity you are able to open to, you will see there are even greater degrees of refined peace and clarity possible.

A very beneficial cycle will have been set in motion.

There does not seem to be any real limit to how far you can go with this beneficial cycle.

5.

Throughout this process of progressing to higher levels of practice and broader reference frames of insight, there is another general theme to apply:

> It is important to honor the serious doubts and unanswered questions you have about what is the truth of this life or the path of liberation you are exploring.

If others do not honor your sincere doubts and unanswered questions, that is their issue to work with. You may need to step back from such people or they may expel you from their group when they find you really don't agree with some of their core doctrines.

In either case it is all the more important to make sure you honor and affirm the value of your doubts and important questions. For it is this process of honoring serious doubts and unanswered questions that will help you find those answers that can be found however paradoxical this approach may seem to be. This is because honoring your doubts is a way of affirming that these doubts are an important and valuable part of your life, which in fact they are. Honoring your doubts is part of the overall process of honoring all the parts of your life and character, even those aspects of character which do need to be changed.

In truth you may or may not ever find some of the answers you seek. But this process of honoring your doubts is a way to change your relationship to and your experience of your doubts and nagging unanswered questions. As you honor and respect your doubts, and live and work with them with a sincere earnestness, you will find they are among your most valuable resources.

The same holds for the truths you feel strongly about.

Honor your truths.

Honor, respect, and live the truths you have found by the way you live your life.

Honor your truths with fidelity and they will continue to generate new life within you.

Surely everyone needs to be open to new ideas and constructive criticism.

But if after careful reflection according to the highest standards of personal integrity and conscience, and the mature counsel of others, you come to believe certain truths or courses of action are very important, then stand your ground.

6.

With regard to mitigating the hard trials of your life, the same gradual and practical process that helps a person work with important unanswered questions will also help resolve painful situations of their life.

Honor your struggles.

Touch the experiences of your struggles with compassionate awareness, care, patience, and acceptance. The same is true for your experiences of joy and triumph. Just this simple practice applied steadily over time will begin to shift your experience of the trials of your life and improve your ability to respond to them.

With regard to the genuine challenges in your life, there may be some you can't do much about in the short term. It is enough to gently but firmly set those challenges aside for the time being.

It is enough to discern which difficult situations or decisions you can do something about in the immediate future that you know you could be making better efforts with.

It is enough to then make the best efforts you reasonably can with those painful life conditions you have a real chance of resolving.

It is enough to find whatever help and resources are available to you and to find the most skillful way to approach any important decisions you may have been putting off.

As you are able to take skillful action and make important decisions, at least some of the difficulties will be assuaged. The general distress you feel will diminish a little bit here and a little bit there. The mind will further calm and clear.

As the mind clears, consciousness will change and purify.

It will be possible to proceed to the next level of practical problem-solving skills available to you. It will be possible to respond more skillfully to the genuine challenges which remain.

At every step of your efforts the following suggestion will help:

> It is important to stop denying that certain problems need your attention, if in fact they do.

It is important to stop hating the fact that you have certain struggles and hardships but rather to do what you can to accept and honor the struggles of your life.

None of this is to imply that it would not be better if these problems never developed.

Nor is it being said that accepting difficult life conditions is some kind of fatalistic resignation. It continues to be important to make the best efforts you reasonably can to change what can and needs to be changed. What is being said is that this acceptance and honoring of the difficulties of your life is the best way to free up reservoirs of energy that were formerly trapped in cycles of denial, resistance, self-pity, or self-reproach.

The suggestion to honor your struggles as well as your triumphs is a vital part of the general process of honoring all the parts of your life as one of the best ways to transform your life experience.

This too is the simple path.

7.

There is a signal benefit to all of the practices that follow. They are presented in such a way that they can be engaged by people whether they do or do not believe in God. After careful consideration, whichever of these two perspectives of belief seems to be most true to you is the right place to begin.

If you really are not sure one way or the other, that is all right too.

Whenever the way forward is unclear let it be unclear.

Let the confusion simply be confusing. As you become more aware of any experiences of being confused, see if you can touch these experiences with awareness, patience, compassion, and acceptance.

A sincere engagement of any practices which are clearly acceptable to you will help generate more in the way of early stages of peace and clarity. The refinements to intuition and insight that arise from such experiences will continue to point to a good general way forward.

You may find yourself inspired to explore some teachings you had previously either rejected or not known much about.

You may find yourself realizing that certain long-held attitudes or beliefs of yours are not really as true or helpful as you once thought they were.

In either case a sincere willingness, supported by reasonable levels of consistent effort over time, to follow the search for truth, wherever it leads, will allow you to find that which you are seeking.

This is a good faith. This is a true faith. This is a simple faith.

Awareness

1.

A more clear awareness of the present moment is the beginning of all silent meditation.

A more clear awareness of each moment is the first true step in the search for wisdom and the means to ameliorate difficult life conditions.

None of this is to imply that one does not think of the future when it is beneficial and enjoyable to do so.

None of this is to imply that one does not think of the past when it is beneficial and enjoyable to do so.

What is being said is that when you decide to focus on the present moment, you learn how to do this for sustained periods of time without the mind drifting off in one distraction or another.

2.

One of the real benefits of silent meditation is that it creates a unique opportunity to clearly see how often your mind drifts off and flits about in one semi-unconscious distraction or another.

While one might think it should be simple enough to sit and maintain one's awareness on their breath or sacred word for the twenty or thirty minutes of their session, this is usually not the case. Most find again and again that after a few seconds or minutes they realize they have drifted off into some new distraction or worry without being aware they had been knocked off their stated intention. Seeing how often the mind drifts off in one distraction after another, or how difficult it is to even sit still and be silent for twenty or thirty minutes, is a good realization to come to.

Why is it so difficult for most of us to keep our mind focused on some simple theme for longer than a few seconds or minutes?

What lessons need to be learned so that one can stay focused on the present moment for more sustained periods of time in the context of the style of meditation they are working with?

What changes in attitudes, beliefs, and behaviors need to happen before a person can calm and clear their mind and settle into the deepest states of awareness and concentration that are possible?

These are important questions and there are very sound and practical answers to these questions.

3.

The reason it is so difficult for most to maintain their awareness on the breath or some sacred word during meditation is that most of us simply are not as conscious or awake as we think we are. Think about it. You decide to sit in stillness and silence with your mind focused on the breath or some sacred word. Then, after a few seconds or minutes, you realize that your mind has drifted off into some thought or concern without your being aware this has happened.

Why does this keep happening?

What are these distractions?

Why can't most of us see them as they arise? Why is it often so difficult to prevent this process of being literally hijacked by these unplanned and unscheduled distractions?

Why is it that most of us realize we have become distracted only after a few seconds or minutes have drifted by, as though we were lost in some interior movie?

If a person was more awake, they would see a thought arising in their mind and be able to make the decision not to get carried away and instead keep their focus on their breath or sacred word.

As a person becomes more fully awake they are able to diffuse the underlying causes which keep forming and sending the stream of distractions in the first place.

Instead, during a meditation session it is as if we keep falling asleep and get carried off by yet another "daydream." Then it is like we wake up and realize we have not been observing the breath or repeating our sacred phrase, and we draw our attention back to the object of our meditation focus.

The goal of meditation is to wake up and to stay awake.

Take the time to find out how often some unplanned and unchosen impulse literally hijacks your mind away from your stated intention to stay focused. Take the time to find out how often you drift off from a clear awareness of the present into some reflection on the future or rumination of the past without making a conscious choice to do so.

Once you realize this is more difficult than you may have imagined, you will gain a sense of one of the many unique values of silent meditation. Since the body is not moving, this simple stillness reduces the number of sensations streaming into the mind. You have already noticeably lessened the overall level of activity and reduced the degree of "charge" to the activity that remains present in your mind. As you further simplify the commotion in the mind it will become more and more possible to observe both the mind and the body more clearly. The same will be true for whatever is happening around you.

As you cultivate the ability to try and stay with each moment under these special conditions, you will begin to observe each moment more clearly. As your skills with this very simple effort develop, you can apply this skill of clear sight more consistently in the moments of the active hours of life as well.

During meditation practice and in the active hours of life it will become more and more possible to see what sensations, emotions, and thoughts arise and pass away as each moment unfolds.

4.

In particular you will begin to observe more clearly any tendencies towards anger, guilt, fear, excessive desire, doubt, vanity, torpor, or illusions that may be active in your life.

It is these particular clusters of stress and agitation that tend to drive a person to make the kinds of unskillful choices that create one complex situation after another. When a person's life is far more complicated and conflicted than necessary, their mind will tend to jump or race from one thought and impulse to another as they try to keep up with the hectic pace of their life.

It is the agitation caused by these particular clusters of stress, and their underlying causes, which are the engines that keep generating the steady stream of distractions you experience.

These particular clusters of stress are the factors which prevent the mind from focusing more steadily and settling into progressively deeper experiences of peace and insight.

As mindful awareness becomes more established and continual, you will be able to observe all the different shades and degrees of anger, guilt, fear, excessive desire, doubt, vanity, torpor, or illusions as they arise and have impact on your mind and body. You will also begin to see these stressful emotions and thoughts in greater detail. This combination of more clear awareness along with far more detailed observations that develop will be very helpful.

You will begin to see the underlying causes that give rise to stress in the first place.

You will then begin to see more clearly the means to diminish the underlying causes of stress and agitation, and you will be able to do so a little bit at a time.

One of the ways this happens is that you will begin to see the formations of such emotions and thoughts in earlier and earlier stages of their formation. As the resources of the mind become stronger and more focused, it becomes more possible to make decisions to diffuse such emotions and thoughts in the early stages of their formation before they gather too much force and momentum. This is a major benefit.

After all, it is easier to put out a small fire than a big one.

5.

As awareness and clarity of mind develop during meditation, it will also be possible to improve practical problem-solving skills and to make more skillful choices. This will lead to a more manageable and stable life.

As one's life becomes more stable, the mind will settle and calm more readily during silent meditation. You will also find that your mind will be more clear in the active hours of life as well. As the mind further clears, you will see additional ways to improve practical problem-solving skills. It will be possible to discern ways to make better use of external resources and the help of others that are available at the time.

It is in these ways that the efforts to be more awake during silent meditation and in the active hours of life affect and complement one another.

6.

Another primary theme of the simple path is to fully recognize it may be very difficult for some people to work with whatever levels of anger, guilt, fear, excessive desire, doubt, vanity, torpor, and illusions that may be active in their life.

The emotional and intellectual intensity of some people's minds is simply more charged and extreme than is the case for others. Also, the painful and disturbing experiences of some people's lives and/ or the biochemistry of their mind are simply more intensely felt and disruptive than is the case for most people.

If this is the case with you, then give yourself permission to proceed at a realistic pace and to be as patient as you can be with any messy, discouraging, and painful setbacks which may arise.

Meditation is no magic wand.

Protracted troubles with finance or romance will not simply melt away. The same is true for serious challenges of physical or mental health, or with very real problems of corruption and violence in the society in which you live.

What high grade skills with meditation can do is help you see any particular situation more clearly and to work with that situation more effectively moment by moment. You will be able to see more clearly what you can do and need to do and what you cannot do in any given moment.

Even so, if you are a slow learner, give yourself permission to be a slow learner, but make the best efforts you reasonably can as steadily as you can over the long contours of your life.

While it makes sense to learn as much as you can from those who are further along or making more rapid progress, you are strongly encouraged not to compete or compare yourself with this one or that one. Some will simply be more gifted or have more favorable conditions in their life. Others will be less gifted or have harder life conditions than is the case for you.

What is important is that you will be amazed what even the slowest learner can learn with simple, sincere, and steady efforts over many years.

7.

The first efforts are to work with any glaring issues with anger, guilt, fear, doubt, excessive desire, vanity, torpor, or illusion that may be active in your life.

Then you can work on the ordinary levels of these kinds of stressful emotions and thoughts that are present to one degree or another in most people's lives.

Finally, it becomes possible to work on the subtle and submerged forms of these conflicted emotions and turbulent thoughts that may be harder to observe and investigate.

As one engages this work, their mind will calm and clear by degree. As the mind clears, one's practical problem-solving skills will also steadily improve. Their life will become more stable and enjoyable. As this work continues, one's intuitive and practical problem-solving skills will become noticeably more effective and both the stability and joy of their life will be further enhanced. Doing the more advanced work of deconstructing even the subtle manifestations of these clusters of stress and agitation will lead to noticeable shifts in your experience of life and your ability to find creative solutions to difficult life conditions.

Step by step, year by year, the fires of suffering will diminish in heat and intensity even if certain arduous life conditions remain or if new troubles arise which are difficult to live and work with.

All this work is offered so a person can learn to do a few very simple things very well:

To wake up and to stay awake.

To be more courageous, joyful, loving, and creative.

To sit in stillness, silence, and emptiness and maintain one's awareness on their breath or sacred word and the present moment for sustained periods of time.

The early-stage experiences of peace and clarity that arise from these simple efforts will help you see a good general direction forward to whatever is the next level of peace and understanding available to you.

When a person has learned how to calm their mind to the degree they do not drift off in one distraction after another, the experiences of peace that will arise will be very, very clear and exceptionally pure. In these states of deep peace and pure consciousness they will become able to perceive the true nature of being.

Even so it is likely that many questions they started with will remain unanswered. But, the consolations of such experiences of peace and clarity will be so refreshing and beautiful that the questions which remain unresolved will be of less and less importance.

Stillness, Silence, and Emptiness

1.

When the subject of meditation comes up, quite a few people say they meditate while they are jogging or gardening but go on to say they have little interest or motivation for sitting in stillness or silence.

This may be as much as they wish to do with meditation and that is fine. Being more clearly aware during one's hobbies and periods of exercise and throughout all of life's errands and work is an important aspect of any effort with meditation. But if this is all you are doing with meditation and you still find any real sense of peace or fulfillment continues to elude you, then you may wish to explore stronger commitments to the practice of stillness and silence.

While practicing awareness during the hours of daily life is good and important, those who need to go deeper, those who want to go deeper, will find the practice of stillness and silence is a uniquely efficacious way to learn and grow. As you learn deeper shades of silence and stillness, the amount of activity in the mind and body is further reduced. As a result of this simplification, greater clarity of thought and intention becomes possible.

2.

It is like a person who has a crowded desk and many phones that keep ringing and a steady stream of people barging into the office.

The practice of stillness and silence is a way to clear the desk, close the door, and unplug the phones so the individual can take the time to look carefully at one issue at a time.

When your body is still, the number of decisions to be made and the number of commands given by the mind is lessened because the body is no longer moving.

When you sit in a quiet place, the number of sensations streaming into the mind through the ears is lessened.

If you sit with your eyes closed or, if you prefer, with the eyes half open and looking directly ahead, the number of sensations streaming into the mind through the eyes is reduced.

If you clear the body of all stimulants, including the petty stimulants of caffeine and sugar, the amount of activity in the nervous system and the blood is lessened. Over time, the nervous system and the blood can come to exist in their most optimal state.

If you gain sufficient control over excessive desires so your digestive tract is as light and clear as good health allows, the mind is not clogged with the countless streams of commands necessary for digestion. Most importantly, the sluggish sensations of being bloated will not arise.

Eliminating any stimulants, gross or petty, and noticeably simplifying the diet is what is meant by the early practices of emptiness which are added to the basic practices of stillness and silence.

Quieting the noisy clamor or stressful emotions and conflicted thoughts is the next general stage of the process of being "empty."

Just these simple things are enough to help slow the mind down so you have a real chance of seeing how the mind acts and reacts. The more clearly you begin to see all the ways the mind acts and reacts then you will also see good and effective ways to further calm your mind and heal the body. Instead of constantly looking outside of yourself, you can now shift the spotlight of your awareness within. You can sit and observe in creative ways more of the dynamics inside your body, heart, and mind.

While the efforts to cultivate mindful awareness need to carry over to all the other activities of life, silent meditation presents a workshop of irreplaceable value.

This workshop is your interior life.

This simplified field of study is the silent interior of your body, heart, and mind.

This simplified field of study is the arising and passing of bodily sensations, emotions, thoughts, plans, schemes, and desires.

3.

In the simplified environment of your interior life some very important vistas come into view.

You will be able to observe the sensations of your body and the emotions and thoughts of your mind far more clearly and precisely. The insights that will arise from this process of observation will help you see which choices and beliefs lead to greater peace and which lead to less peace.

You will begin to see more clearly and in increasing detail any experiences of dissatisfaction and suffering. You will begin to see with greater clarity the underlying causes and the best means to diminish the underlying causes of dissatisfaction and suffering. You will also begin to discover from where you can find more of the interior resources needed to make whatever changes you need to make in your life. The same is true for any external resources and help available to you which you previously missed, overlooked, or rejected.

You can also find out what it is like to just be you.

You can find out what it is that catches up with you when you are no longer running in so many directions. In fact, it is in this regard that working with a competent guide is particularly important. Once you stop running so fast in so many different directions, certain anxieties and stresses that were sort of pushed below the level of consciousness by all this commotion will begin to surface into conscious experience. Having the right guide and friends, should you be fortunate enough to find such people, are important sources of support when this happens. They can offer support and guidance about how to process any of these anxieties and conflicts. They can also help you work with any glimpses into those unflattering aspects of character which may come into view now that you are seeking to face your life more cleanly and openly.

This is a good thing. Developing your own abilities to see more clearly and finding one or two people you can trust to help you see the "blind spots" of your character, attitudes, and behaviors are essential efforts to commit to. What is important to understand is that quite a bit of patience may be needed as you search for people who are both skillful and trustworthy.

4.

As you begin to understand and trust there is a lasting value to sitting in stillness, silence, and emptiness you will be more willing to make this practice a higher priority. You will be more willing to find ways to simplify your life and enhance your discipline so you can meditate on a very regular basis.

For good or bad reasons, it may take a while before you can really perceive this value or make the changes you wish you could make so that you would have more time for daily practice.

Be as patient as you can yet work diligently to gain the understanding and trust needed to believe these efforts will be very beneficial for your life.

Even greater efforts with patience may be needed if you are living with serious problems such as physical or emotional health concerns, money problems, broken romantic aspirations, or if you are in the early stages of recovery from trauma or addiction. There simply may be little time or energy available for silent meditation. If this is the case for you, the following will help.

If you have no time for meditation or just can't seem to sit still for a few minutes, it is enough to simply look more clearly and openly at each moment of the active hours of your life. Over time, this basic practice will give rise to the insights that will help you perceive the value of proceeding to less hurried efforts.

The same is true if the conditions of your life are more favorable yet you have built up a complex life with many stressful responsibilities that genuinely need to be met. As a result of competitive expectations of family and society, many people have built up a more complex life of family, work, and community responsibilities than they may have intended. For many, the stress of these responsibilities takes a toll and they begin to wish for a simpler life. But the responsibilities of work and family that have been made are genuine and need to be met. If this is a general description of your life, there may also not be much time for study and silent meditation other than occasional efforts.

This will help.

You can transition to a simpler life gradually over time.

As your commitments to work or family responsibilities are met, and as a greater understanding of the value of silent meditation coalesces, it will be possible to make some changes in your life. It will be possible to practice at least occasionally and then, at some point, on a daily basis and to be more consistently mindful during the active hours of your life.

None of this is to imply that one should not make the efforts they reasonably can to develop a daily meditation practice assuming they have any general interest in meditation to begin with.

What is being said is that you can start with the simplest of efforts no matter how difficult or harried your life may be.

Do the little bit that you can, and then a little more.

This is the simple path.

5.

Please don't be too discouraged or surprised if after one or two or a dozen sittings there are no great visions or profound experiences of peace and insight.

This is no more likely than it would be for a beginning piano student to play an advanced piece of music after only a few lessons. Besides, despite the captivating stories of raptures and visions one reads or hears about, these only happen to a few people no matter what a person tries to do or agrees to believe. Furthermore, the most mature commentators through history have been consistent in saying that the spiritual life is not about raptures or visions however fulfilling such experiences may be.

The spiritual life is about waking up and being a more loving and decent human being.

The spiritual life is the process of making a sincere search for a creative vision of life and faith you can freely accept and commit to and then embracing that vision with as much integrity and fidelity as you can.

What is available to everyone are increasingly deeper levels of peace, clarity, maturity, and wisdom. With or without visions or raptures, you can depend on the fact that the deepening consolations that arise from these personal changes will heal and satisfy the deepest wishes of the heart. Still, just as a beginning piano student will play some simple melodies that are quite enchanting, early-stage experiences of peace and clarity will arise which will confirm you are moving in a good general direction.

Searching for good teachers and friends who can share this practice with you will be of real help as you seek to cultivate commitment and discipline. But finding a teacher and a circle of friends that you can really benefit from and get along with may not be so easy especially for those people who tend to walk on the boundaries or fringes of the established traditions.

One problem is that a lot of meditation teachers do not have a wide range of skills. Many really do not know how to help people who have serious doubts and unanswered questions or whose emotions surge more strongly than most, or whose life conditions are just much harder and messier than others. Also, a substantial number who offer meditation instruction do not have the time, interest, or skills needed to help a person resolve the difficult situations in their life that need to be tended to before a serious practice of meditation can really commence.

Even worse, more than a few are con-artists who are just out for the money and an easy ride.

6.

Another problem for many people is that almost all traditions of meditation instruction are deeply enmeshed with various religious teachings or views of life. It is not just that substantial portions of these teachings are not true; the problem is many are wrong and damaging.

This comment from a meditation written in 1897 is a good, if somewhat extreme, example of how far off a good path even a courageous and exemplary monk such as Charles de Foucauld can occasionally drift in their spiritual reflections and commentary.

> " 'Thinking about death': Remember that you ought to die as a martyr, stripped of everything, stretched naked on the ground, unrecognizable, covered with wounds and blood, killed violently and painfully, and desire that it be today."[1]

1   Charles de Foucauld, *Writings Selected with an Introduction by Robert Ellsberg*, Maryknoll, New York: Orbis Books, 1999, p 77.

There are many, many more selections from east and west that could be cited as troubling passages in commentaries on meditation and the spiritual search.

When you come across such jarring passages, set them aside as best you can.

If you find you really cannot understand or accept a lot of what you hear at certain meditation centers or monasteries, then persevere on your own until you find more mature people to practice with.

It is enough to learn what you can and to draw what consolations and fellowship you can from those you meet.

If you are more or less not on the same wavelength as whatever is the prevailing "group-think," it is best not to ask too many questions let alone to argue with the teachers or fellow students of various group-think-tribes. They will not have the time or interest to deal with anyone who is not more or less committed to what they are offering. This is especially true if you are asking questions for which they don't know the answers. Still, here and there, some may agree with you in private that there are important inconsistencies in some of what they are saying or some of what is written in their sacred books. But they will not be willing to really think through the implications of certain inconsistencies even if they basically agree with some of what you are saying. To do more than just agree in private would mean they would have to fully address the inconsistencies they have based major portions of their life and identity upon. However valuable such a tipping over of the apple cart may be, only a few are detached enough to actually admit they no longer really believe in major portions of what they have built their life upon. Furthermore, for many spiritual teachers, their truths are really just the props for their authority, prestige, and control. Regardless of how nice and friendly they may appear to be, if you challenge the foundations of what they have based their privileged position and hidden self-serving conceits upon, you will quickly find out what really is important to them.

But, assuming you are sincere in your willingness to follow truth where the search for truth leads, sooner or later you will find others who are dedicated and more skillful and more open-minded. Why this is true may not be exactly known, but it does seem to be true.

You will know a good teacher in this way:

> There will be a natural joy and kindness about them even though they will be the first to admit there is still a lot of work they are doing in their personal practice and search for deeper faith.

> They will have an unusual blend of personal strength and tenderness, of real courage and genuine humility. They will be patient and willing to work with the messy aspects of human relations.

> When they sit in meditation it will be evident they are very, very calm and silent within.

> They will not need you to agree with them unless you freely do agree. Rather they will be interested to find out what path you are on and to see if they can be of help.

> If they cannot be of help, they will tell you this openly and with kindness, and wish you well. Hopefully, they will also be able to at least point you in the right direction of someone who can be of help.

> If they can be of help, they will expect you to express a reasonable level of deference and respect for their greater proficiency and experience as they endeavor to share those insights that they feel are most true.

> They will never, never ask you to agree with something they say just because they or someone else insists that you agree.

7.

Still, while the search continues for the right teacher and circle of friends, there is much that can be learned from those who are generally respectable people but with whom you simply disagree on important matters. Just the truly excellent discipline and skills of many such teachers and students will help you make greater commitments to the discipline and consistency of your efforts. Even if you don't quite fit into their community or share their views on certain important topics, you can still draw inspiration from the positive aspects of their witness.

The books and commentaries of the great monastic traditions of the world are another source of inspiration for the dissident pilgrim, even if quite a few of the comments in even the most venerable of these books are truly damaging and need to be set aside.

Such comments about St. John of the Cross, "We hear repeatedly that St. John of the Cross desired nothing for himself but to suffer and be despised," is another good example of a comment that needs to be set aside even though many other teachings of this saint are of great value.[2]

Another example is this comment by St. Teresa Benedicta of the Cross as she wrote about the life of St. Teresa Margaret of the Sacred Heart, "Indeed, she did not shrink from inflicting severe penances on her sensitive body."[3]

This comment was made as part of a favorable review of St. Teresa Margaret's vocation without any comment whatsoever about the misguided nature of such a practice. The way the comment was made clearly seems to endorse such practices. Also omitted is any serious reflection as to why this young woman who entered her

---

2   *The Collected Works of Edith Stein Volume 4 The Hidden Life*, edited by Dr. L. Gelber and Michael Linssen O.C.D., Washington, DC: ICS Publications, 1992, p 91.

3   Ibid. p 69.

convent in good health but then subsequently died within a few years. The question never seems to have been asked, "Did the underlying emotional state and social culture which supported such 'severe penances' play a contributing role in weakening the overall health of this young woman, and many others like her?"

For another example, there is a story attributed to Gautama, as relayed by Bhante Gunaratana, that compares acting upon sexual impulses to what happens when lepers touch their wounds with burning logs as a way to get the itching to stop. The result and moral of this unwholesome parable is that the lepers were badly burned *and their itching only got worse.* What is unfortunate about such an unwholesome image is that so much of the rest of this commentary by Bhante Gunaratana is truly excellent.[4]

Still the discipline and the humanity that shines through the lives and better passages of these kinds of commentaries will continue to affirm the value of prayer and meditation in ways that inspire you to cultivate similar levels of skill and commitment.

The sacred art, music, and architecture of many monasteries and retreat centers will also inspire you to realize there is something magnificent to be experienced by a full commitment to stillness, silence, and emptiness. Many people find it much easier to learn from the buildings, art, and music of religions than it is from their sacred books or priests. Others are glad to fully participate in the study of scriptures and the rituals and sacraments of worship.

Find what works for you.

Set aside that which does not feel to be right.

Be open to seeing what various churches, monasteries, or meditation centers have to offer.

---

4   Bhante Gunaratana, *Eight Mindful Steps to Happiness*, Boston: Wisdom Publications, 2001, pgs 119-120.

Remember you do not need to agree with everything they say to find there are many teachings and experiences that prove to be very helpful. But if in your search you encounter covert dysfunction or raw hypocrisy beneath the smiles, then withdraw if you feel you need to.

Sacred Exercise

1.

Sacred forms of exercise such as Yoga or T'ai Chi will not only help heal and tone the body. These forms of exercise are practices in meditation and mindful awareness in their own right. They are also excellent preparations for silent meditation.

This healing and toning of the body will also disperse the conditions that generate torpor which is best defined as a sluggish and dull mind. Torpor, or ennui, or a general sense of malaise, are hindrances that will prevent a person from moving forward.

Look carefully at the body.

You will be amazed at how complex, intricate, and subtle the body is.

Look carefully at the body.

As you seek to do some basic stretching exercises, prior to meditation, notice where the body may be sore and tight and how sore it is.

This will give you an idea how sore and constricted the emotions and conflicted the thought-structures in the mind may be as well.

As you are able to heal and tone the body, this will also lead to a more supple and relaxed mind, although it may take quite a bit of patience to work through any serious health issues you are experiencing. These forms of exercise also help the breath settle into a good and steady rhythm and this too will help you prepare for times of silence, stillness, and emptiness.

Wilderness hiking or swimming or other forms of general exercise are other good choices. But the subtleties of Yoga or T'ai Chi and like practices are uniquely suited to heal the body. These disciplines help by restoring a healthy flow of blood throughout the body, improving the quality of the digestive process, and refining the energy fields of the nervous system.

A slower, steadier rhythm to the breath and a more relaxed body and mood tone are all very practical and beneficial preparations for meditation. The same is true for positive experiences with therapeutic massage.

These efforts all contribute to an overall enhancement of the tone and quality of life, health, and stamina, all of which are needed for serious effort.

2.

The same is true for talk and other forms of art or expressive mental health therapy. Talking openly and freely with a mature and knowledgeable person about emotional stresses or practical problems, and being mindful as one does so, will also help diminish stress in the mind and body.

For those who suffer from more severe mental health conditions, there are many cases where medication can help a person come to a more stable functionality and sense of well-being. These enhancements have the additional benefit that they help the person seeking recovery from impaired biochemistry or neurological conditions to engage other forms of treatment more effectively. If someone who is properly trained and knowledgeable of all your life conditions suggests that such medications may be needed, it is worth giving their recommendations serious consideration. This is assuming they are making these recommendations in the context of a well- rounded program of treatment and not just writing prescriptions because that is the only way they get paid by the insurance companies.

This is also assuming such a person has well-developed skills with meditation and a view of life that seems well thought out and generally consistent with your values and standards or integrity.

Seeking out mental health counseling, if needed, to find some additional ways to heal and calm the mind as part of the overall preparation for silent meditation is a positive step for many. The problem with such efforts is that the mental health sciences are still in a far earlier stage of development than many trained care-givers will admit or are aware of. It can be just as difficult to find a skilled care-giver in these helping professions as it can be to find a meditation teacher who has a well-rounded approach. Furthermore, too many professionally employed care-givers either do not have a well-developed vision of life and faith, or if they do, are too quick to seek to impose their vision of life and faith on others. Finding a care-giver who has the right degree of experience and yet who also respects your vision of life to the degree that you have one, may not be easy to do, but it is good to keep searching for such people. Perhaps as you proceed and find out how few such people actually exist, you may feel called to become someone who can be of help to those who are still very much confused and searching for healing.

3.

There is another general issue with many traditions of meditation instruction that needs to be touched upon.

In both eastern and western cultures there are long standing predispositions to view and describe the body and the ordinary desires of the body in very negative terms. The fact that these life-negating attitudes are dissolving in favor of life-affirming views of the body and the world is one of the most helpful trends in the ancient and modern spiritual cultures of the world. When you read such negative comments in old or modern commentaries on meditation, or hear them in some meditation talk, it is important to be aware of what is being said. It is important not to underestimate the unhealthy impact such comments can have if you do not dismiss them quickly.

There are many commentaries on exercise one can study and many centers and spas where one can cultivate high-grade skills with Yoga, T'ai Chi, and the like. What is helpful to keep in mind is that almost all such commentaries and forms of sacred exercise in these centers or spas are tied to complex teachings on religion and human destiny.

Some may find the related teachings of any one of these various places to be quite helpful. If this is the case for you, then you are fortunate for you have found your path to walk.

But, if you find the teachings and viewpoints at such centers or spas to be confusing, or ridiculous, or vague, or downright dysfunctional, then pay attention to your "gut" reactions. It is safe to say that in the majority of cases you will be right. If this is the case, you can decide whether the benefits of the center you are visiting outweigh the negatives enough to continue or if it would be better to move on.

The sexual abuse of devotees by a primary teacher in the 1990s at the well-known Yoga Spa Kripalu in Massachusetts is one vivid example of the raw dysfunction of many gurus ensconced at what are otherwise very high-grade spas or reputable yoga centers. There are many, many other such distressing examples.

It is enough to trust your gut impressions as you visit such places and to maintain a healthy degree of skepticism until you have a clearer impression of what is really being offered. As a general rule, any center or spa you visit where there are more than a couple of pictures of the senior teachers of that spa displayed is a clear indication it is wise to keep your guard up. While it may not be true in all settings, anywhere you see pictures of a mortal teacher widely displayed is a sign that someone is trying to create a cult of personality.

It is best to compassionately set aside any teachings and any teachers you find to be either confusing or manipulative or downright wrong. Over time you may return to those teachings and teachers you have left behind if you come to realize there is more value in such resources than you previously thought. This is assuming you are not using a general cynicism and skepticism as a defensive shield which precludes any real engagement with life or chance to learn new and valuable information.

The basics of learning how to refine your diet and to heal and tone the body through sacred exercise will serve you well.

The same is true for whatever efforts may be needed to cultivate mental health, well-being, and awareness.

The Basics of Meditation Practice

1.

It is helpful to set aside a little area of your home that is the place where you practice meditation. If your home is a bit larger, you may be fortunate to have a whole room you can set aside as a small private chapel.

You may wish to display certain pictures, statues, or symbols that are meaningful to you as a way to make this place beautiful. If such imagery is not consistent with your faith tradition, that is all right as well. There are other ways to beautify and sacralize your place of practice such as attractive plants or creative designs that have no particular image.

2.

As noted in the preceding chapter, some general limbering exercises as a prelude to silent meditation such as Yoga or T'ai Chi will definitely help soothe the mind and body.

The steady rhythmic breathing of such exercises will allow the breath to slow a bit and be more refined as you begin your meditation session. The body and the mind will also already be a bit more calm than when you left the job site or office.

3.

Whether you sit cross-legged on a cushion or in a regular sitting position in a chair is not so important.

What is important is that if you sit in a chair, it is best not to lean against the back of the chair or rest your arms on the armrest. It is important to sit upright with the back straight, though not rigidly so.

What is also important is to be generally aware of your posture during your meditation sessions and in the active hours of life as well. The practice of being aware of your posture is another good way to cultivate awareness and insight. As you look more closely at your posture you can gain some insights as to how your posture is a manifestation of confident, unconfident, defensive, or swaggering perspectives of life.

A good and upright posture in life and meditation is a good way to express an alert and healthy acceptance and engagement of life. If your shoulders are rounded and if you find you are slouching during meditation, this is something to work on during your exercise activities. It may take a while to strengthen the legs, abdomen, and back so you can sit upright for a full meditation session. If your shoulders are rounded and if your back is slouching it may also take a while to loosen the shoulder and neck muscles so you can draw the head and shoulders back so you can sit with good posture. The same general call to patience applies to the efforts to open any sore and constricted areas of the body that are the constituent parts of poor general posture.

No doubt the general attitudes in a person's life which affect their posture developed over many years during their youth and adolescence. It follows that seeking to improve posture in young adulthood or middle-age will probably also take quite a bit of time. This is especially true if you find your neck and shoulders or other parts of your body are quite sore and stiff.

For those living with chronic physical pain, it is understood that any of this work will be quite a bit more difficult and only partially effective. What is important is to keep searching. *There have to be better ways we can learn to diminish chronic physical pain.* What is known is that the basics of all these practices will help a person change their relationship to the pain they are living with and this will shift the experience of their pain. This alone will diminish many aspects that had added to the sharpness of the sting they had been feeling. One of the most important areas of research in contemplative studies is to explore how more diligent applications of the basic practices can further our understanding of how to help people diminish the tyranny of chronic physical pain. If you are struggling with these particular challenges, please know the best wishes possible are offered that you or someone you know can make real progress with these areas of contemplative and medical research.

Difficult as it may be to heal and open the body, the current health and posture of your body and your current understanding of life, medicine, and suffering is what you have to work with. If the challenges you face are genuinely difficult, you will have to be even more patient and gentle with yourself and, if possible, with others. It will be all the more important to work as skillfully as possible with the basics of compassion, acceptance, and perseverance as you seek spiritual and medical knowledge to ameliorate painful life conditions.

What can any of us do but begin or begin again from where we are now?

Do the little that you can and then a little more.

Seek out others with common challenges. See in what ways you can help one another.

4.

If you want to explore how meditation can help you find more peace, but don't ever seem to have the time or simply do not make good use of the time that is available, don't be too discouraged. What is important is to do what you reasonably can to free up the time needed and to make better use of the time which is available for serious intention.

Cultivating a more clear awareness during the active hours of your life will get the ball rolling. Even if this is all you can or are willing to do, this will prove to be a decisive beginning.

As you seek to observe each moment more honestly, openly and clearly you will begin to see ways to make changes and improve disciplined effort over time. Sooner or later this will allow you to dedicate more unhurried time for silence and stillness.

If you can't sit for twenty minutes then sit for five or two. If this is the case, then be open to increasing the length of the sessions as soon as you reasonably can. Taking the pressure off by not thinking you need to force yourself to sit for longer periods of time may be enough to ease into sitting for at least a few minutes. Giving yourself permission to sit for just a few minutes may well be enough to have at least a modest time of meditation before each day starts. You may find that by not blowing off the time for meditation altogether you may be able to sit for a longer duration once you do sit down. These are some of the practical methods one can use almost as ways to trick one's self into sitting in stillness and silence for at least a few minutes. This may well be enough to help you establish at least a modest daily meditation practice. When you are ready, you can proceed from there. These comments are offered with the assumption that the constraints of time and schedule are real and not just an excuse to avoid making a good quality effort.

Going on an occasional weekend retreat is another catalyst to establishing more discipline and consistency to your practice. Finding a meditation group at a local church or center that you can go to will also help, if you can find such a group or center where you can accept the rest of the teachings they offer as part of their meditation instruction. Again, even if you are not sure of some of the core teachings offered at such places, the discipline of sitting with others for the full duration of a meditation session or retreat will help you develop more consistent practice.

For those who have more time and discipline, it is wise to be grateful for this time and willingness, for you are fortunate indeed. When you are ready to be of help to others, you can help inspire them to greater efforts by the steadfastness of your practice. This will help both you and them.

5.

The breath is not the only choice of focus for meditation. Many prefer some simple word or phrase or sacred image they are drawn to venerate in a devotional way. They find that trying to focus on the breath alone is a bit too difficult. They find the word and thought centers of their mind need a word or phrase or image to concentrate upon as a focal point of mental organization.

Others prefer the breath as their meditation focus because it is not tied to any words or concepts or system of theology. Also, the breath is always present except in fairly rare medical conditions or emergencies as a center of focus.

Many traditions such as the Greek and Russian Orthodox which favor a sacred word or phrase make the suggestion that you try to match the syllables of a sacred word or phrase to the rhythm of the breath as you breathe in and out. Many of these traditions also offer the following suggestion: As the meditation session proceeds and you notice the mind and breathing have slowed and quieted, you can cease the repetition of the words and just be present to the breath and the wordless moment.

The choice in these matters is completely up to you in the context of the tradition you are studying. In this commentary, for the sake of simplicity, the focus of meditation is referenced as the breath, actually the point where the breath passes the top of the upper lip and the rim of the nostrils as the narrow focus of concentration practice. *When you read a reference to the breath in this commentary please feel free to interpret this as referring to whichever sacred word, phrase, or image you have chosen.*

What is important is that you choose a simple theme to focus on and to stick with that theme day in and day out, year in and year out, unless for some good and thoughtful reason you decide to choose a different theme. But if you do make a change then stick with that new choice for a good long while. Constantly changing the theme of your awareness and concentration practice will not be helpful. Making a clear choice and steady commitments as to what is the theme of your meditations will help. You will never have to guess what you are going to do in your session. You can just begin as you usually do. This continuity of a well-chosen practice will help generate momentum in your practice.

6.

When you begin a meditation session, it is helpful to take a few moments to shift back and forth a bit to make sure you are in a position that you can hold for the time of your meditation. When you feel you have settled into a sustainable position, then commit to being still during the time of meditation. If some true emergency arises then simply get up and respond to whatever needs to be tended to. Other than a real emergency, however, it is helpful to commit to being as still as you can for the time you set aside.

It is also helpful to note whether the mind is already fairly calm or whether there is quite a bit of tension and racing thought.

Give yourself the permission to let the mood and present set of conditions be what they are as you draw your attention to the breath and enter the session.

If the breath is a little shallow and choppy, then let it be shallow and choppy.

If the breath is slow and measured, then let it be slow and measured.

But, if the inhale and exhale are fairly quick and shallow there is not quite as much for one to observe. Still the focus should be to observe what detail you can of the sensations of the breath when your breathing is fairly quick and shallow.

When the mind wanders, or you feel some itch on your chin, or you shift your awareness to the changes in the abdomen as you breathe, then simply draw your attention back to the sensations of the breath in the nostrils.

Sooner or later, either today or tomorrow or next week or month, the breath will slow at least a bit and then a little bit more.

Don't try to force the breath to slow down other than by living as simply as you can or doing some relaxing exercises beforehand so the breath is already a bit slower and the mind a bit more calm as you begin a session. Just try to keep observing what you can of the breath and *be open to the breath slowing to the silken and refined texture that is possible.*

As the breath slows, the mind and heartbeat will follow.

As the breath slows noticeably, it becomes possible to see that each cycle of the breath has many micromoments. It is the attention to an increasing level of minute detail of the sensations of the breath that creates the chance for concentrated awareness that is more sustained and which is interrupted less and less frequently by distractions.

The following detailed description of the moments and micromoments of the cycle of the breath will be helpful as you seek to cultivate this sustained awareness.

There are the sensations of the breath at the place where the upper lip meets the rim of the nostrils at the beginning of the inhale and there are the sensations at this point during the rest of each inhale.

There are the sensations at the top of the inhale when you are no longer inhaling but neither has the exhale really begun.

Then there are the sensations of the beginning of the exhale. Then there is the fading of the sensations of the exhale and finally the end of the exhale when there is barely any sensation of the breath or air in the nostrils at all.

There is the pause at the bottom of the exhale when it is finished yet before the next inhale has begun. This pause will tend to be longer than the pause at the top of the inhale and this period of the breath cycle presents very real challenges. With little to no sensation it may be quite difficult to maintain direct awareness of the place where the upper lip meets the opening of the nostrils until there is a new inhale.

Since there are so few sensations during this pause at the bottom of the exhale you may need to develop some secondary focus such as the pulse of the heartbeat you notice in the face or to count the breaths one at a time at the bottom of each exhale. If you decide to do this, it is important also to try to remain focused on any faint presence of the air in and around the rim of the nostrils. By doing this your steady awareness can remain unbroken until the beginning of the next inhale occurs. Most find it is during the inhale that is the easiest time to maintain mindful awareness. The more proficient you become, the more you will notice a finer range of detail of the sensations at the top of the upper lip and the opening to the nose. As this finer, more nuanced awareness develops, you will no longer need any secondary focus to shift to at the bottom of the exhale. As soon as possible, it is best to let go of any second point of awareness during the long hiatus when the exhale has more or less ended and the inhale has not begun again.

As you learn to stay with the sensations in the nostrils of the full cycle of the breath you will begin to notice there will be points in the cycle of the breath where it is more likely to get hijacked by some unscheduled distraction. As you develop your concentrated awareness, can you make an effort to be extra vigilant at the top of the breath as you begin the exhale and during the fading of the sensations as the exhale is completed?

Can you especially remain more focused at the bottom of the exhale in the period of a few seconds before the next inhale has started? If you can maintain an extra focus during the transition points of each part of the cycle of each breath, it is more likely you will be able to maintain your awareness without distraction. It is important not to try to force this process too much. Finding the right balanced effort that is neither too driven nor too lax may be a bit tricky but it is this balance you are looking for.

Some find it helpful to count breaths from one to a hundred as a way of maintaining their concentration. This counting gives the word-thought center of the mind something to do other than breed distractions. But this too may work only for a while. When you realize you have forgotten where you are in the count or if you are not really sure if you remember the last number you were on, then start again at one.

In other traditions emphasis is placed on counting the number of distractions experienced during the time of sitting meditation and noticing whether the number of distractions is increasing or decreasing. In other traditions, when the practitioner becomes aware they have become distracted, they simply make the mental note, "Thinking," and come back to the breath.

See which of these methods seems to be the most effective for you.

And above all be patient. This work is more difficult than it seems.

Really, be patient. This work can be a lot more difficult than it sounds at first.

7.

When you enter a meditation session, leave the cares of the day, as best you can, outside the door of your room like shoes outside a meditation hall.

Take the time to learn how to set aside the cares, pressures, and excessive desires of the day for a while even if it takes quite a bit of stumbling to learn how to do this.

Take the time to learn to set aside all of your plans, schemes, and agendas during your meditation regardless of whether they are worthy or self-centered in some gross or petty way.

Let the general experience of the self become smaller, humbler, and more general.

Take the time also to set aside the needs and concerns of <u>all</u> other people for the period of your meditation and reflection regardless of whether those needs of others are genuine or spurious.

It is not that meditation is some way of hiding from or running away from the world or the responsibilities of life and community. *Meditation is a way of stepping back from the ordinary ways of doing and thinking so that one can find new ways to be refreshed at a very deep level.*

You can count on the fact that both the genuine and spurious concerns of your life and the needs of other people will all still be there when your meditation session has ended. But, when you return to the legitimate responsibilities of your own life and the needs of others you will be able to do so with fresh, clear energy, and steadily increasing levels of skill.

8.

In the beginning or middle or end of any particular session give yourself the permission to let the mood and present conditions be what they are.

If you are relaxed then be relaxed.

If you are tense and uncomfortable then be tense and uncomfortable. If the sun is shining, let it shine. If the conditions are unfavorable, let them be unfavorable.

If you have serious doubts about God or religious teachings or whether there is any such thing as truth or meaning in this world, then let that be all right as well. If you are bored out of your mind, then observe the boredom and restlessness and see if you can remember the high purpose you have hoped to attain with these efforts.

It is enough to sit in stillness, silence, and emptiness.

It is enough to honor the doubts you have and to touch your felt experiences of doubt and confusion with a tender acceptance, patience, and compassion.

All of this is good basic practice of letting go of any clumsy attempts to force your experience of the present moment into being something other than it clearly is.

None of this is to imply that one should not make the best efforts they can to ameliorate painful interior states or external life conditions. After all, the foundations of what Buddhists refer to as Right Effort (one of the practices of the Eight-Fold path) are to make the skillful effort to substitute wholesome states for those which are unwholesome and to make the most skillful moral choices in any given situation.

What is being said is to see and fully experience what is happening in the present moment and to accept those interior states or external conditions which can't be readily changed and essentially to wait them out.

The great paradox is that this concentrated awareness, and clear seeing, and acceptance of what cannot be changed will give rise to the skills needed to more effectively change the things you can.

Concentration and Insight Practice

1.

The phrase "mindful awareness" is better known in contemporary western meditation circles than is the phrase "concentration practice."

This is due mostly to the fact that the traditions of Buddhist meditation which emphasize "mindful awareness" were established on a wider basis in the west than were those which emphasize "concentration practice." Having noted that the phrases "mindful awareness" and "concentration practice" are translations of terms drawn from Buddhist tradition, it is important to add that one does not need to become a Buddhist to engage these practices unless you wish to do so. Many may find that some teachings of Buddhism are neither appealing nor true. Still, these practices of mindful awareness and concentration are better developed in the Buddhist and Hindu cultures than is the case with most other meditation traditions. Furthermore, they are basic and neutral enough that they can be adapted to any other style of meditation or study of ethics which have a genuinely moral tone and high standards of personal integrity.

Before reflecting on the ways concentration practices are a bit different from mindful awareness it is important to acknowledge that concentration is a form of mindful awareness. It just happens to be a further development of mindful awareness.

As for the differences of nuance between mindful awareness and concentration practice:

> First, concentration is the extension of mindful awareness without interruption over a sustained period of time.

> Second, the focus of concentration practice tends to be more narrowly drawn than the more general practice of being aware of whatever is happening in any particular moment.

A good example is this: focusing on the place where the breath passes the top of the upper lip and the rim of the nostrils is a much more narrowly drawn focus than a shifting awareness of a wide variety of different sensations of the body.

2.

As is the case with almost any important spiritual practice, there are a number of options how each person can best cultivate concentration. It might be preferable if there was one general choice that works for everyone, but that is not the case. Different people have different aptitudes and temperaments and so a wider range of choices is needed. While these options have many areas where the efforts overlap, discerning which option is most efficacious for you is a discernment that can be made gradually as one proceeds.

The first option is what has generally been alluded to in the past few chapters and is the general focus of almost all general introductions to meditation. This option is to endeavor to focus on a narrowly drawn point for sustained periods of time without drifting off in a semi-unconscious state in one distraction after another.

A full development of this skill is called "single point concentration."

In other words the mind is focused on a single point without distraction. This practice is also commonly referred to as "absorption" or "Samadhi" in eastern religions. This particular type of meditation is a foundation practice of many monastic cultures, but is especially pronounced in Theravada (Vipassana) Buddhism and the Raja (or Astanga) tradition of Yoga in Hinduism.

The experiences of peace and clarity that arise from this highly concentrated state are exceptionally pure and refreshing and for this reason are highly attractive. Unfortunately there is an open question as to whether this degree of concentration is really attainable by all who are willing to work towards this goal with reasonable levels of diligence.

While it seems possible that with better means of instruction this single point concentration could be attained by any intelligent person with a decent work ethic, if after sustained efforts this does not quite come together that is not the end of the story. Gautama clearly stated that single point concentration is not essential to attain enlightenment, although it is a skill he cultivated to a high degree. Certainly Christian teachers would concur that deep states of contemplative prayer are not essential to salvation however much such experiences help a person find peace in this life.

The reason that any inherent limits to one's natural aptitudes with single point concentration are not critical limitations is because advanced states of concentration are not ends in themselves. They are one means to cultivate the insights needed for liberation. The same is true for exalted and rarified states of peace. They too are not ends in themselves. They too are one set of means to cultivate the insights needed to pierce the illusions that keep one bound.

There are other pathways that do not quite require the cultivation of single point concentration, or the advanced degrees of concentration which follow. In these alternative paths it is enough to still develop the best skills with concentration one reasonably can. What is important is that these other trails also lead to the summit. They just may not be quite as direct. What is also important is that the vistas which open on these other trails can also be stunningly beautiful and deeply satisfying.

3.

The primary alternative to single point concentration, and the advanced states of concentration which follow, is a slightly different variation of mindfulness referred to as "Insight Meditation." This form of Buddhist meditation is also commonly known in America and parts of Western Europe as "Vipassana Meditation." All these terms are derived from the Theravada Buddhist tradition which is the original school developed from Gautama's practice and by his disciples. This school of Buddhist meditation is now most widely practiced in Ceylon, Burma, Thailand, and other parts of Southeast Asia.

In this form of practice, there is less of a need to try to diffuse all distractions or to focus exclusively on one narrow point to the exclusion of all others.

The sustained act of concentrated intention is to be aware of whatever is arising and to make a conscious choice about what particular phenomenon one will choose to observe and investigate.

What is different about this form of practice from more ordinary levels of semi-unconscious awareness is this: while the focus of awareness may continue to shift from one point to another, the mind is fully alert and awake as these decisions are made. The mind does not drift hazily off to another point without realizing that it is moving on.

It is not that distractions are completely forestalled, for some still arise. But the distractions that do arise come with much less frequency and force than is the case with ordinary states of confusion and stress. This is because the high intermediate skills with general concentration practice that anyone is capable of are still effective at significantly quieting and clearing the mind. These high intermediate skills are referred to as "access" or "neighboring" concentration. This is because they are the threshold through which one accesses single point concentration or that one is in the "neighborhood" of single point concentration.

In a state of confused or agitated awareness, it is as if the sky is covered with heavy grey clouds. There is no sight of the sun and the days are generally quite gloomy. Access or neighboring concentration, on the other hand, is like a day when the sun is clearly shining but there are a few puffy clouds drifting by. While the sky is not as completely clear as is the case with single point concentration, it is still a very beautiful and peaceful day.

In the high intermediate states of concentration and insight practice, the awake and alert mind simply sees the distractions as they arise. The difference is one does not get lost or swept away by these distractions but watches mindfully as they arise, peak, break apart, and pass away.

As one becomes proficient with this insight practice, the effort is to look carefully at each new phenomenon to see what can be learned. Another choice is to simply watch as though one was sitting on a high mountain ridge observing in detail the changes of weather as they blow through the valley.

The benefits and rewards of this practice may be different in nuance than those of advanced states of concentration but they are very real and satisfying all the same. The mind is very alert, bright, and joyful. The heart is very calm, spacious, and open. The body is very still, relaxed, and calm. This practice draws its name from a very simple process. The more clearly one can observe whatever is happening, the more readily they will learn that all experiences have a few features in common. Learning what features all experiences have in common allows one to gain the insights needed to let go of the ordinary attachments and excessive desires that prevent a person from being free. What those common features are, as taught by the Theravada Buddhist tradition, is a subject explored in outline form in the last chapter "Insight and Illusion."

In some ways insight practice is a great freedom compared to the efforts of attaining single point concentration. With insight practice one is not as stringently focused on diffusing all distractions, but rather is open to observe whatever sensations, emotions, and thoughts that arise. None of this is to imply that the ordinary moral constraints of what are and are not wholesome thoughts to entertain are somehow suspended and "anything goes." This is not the case. The general constraints of what is and is not a wholesome thought to entertain remain in effect.

But there is a great freedom to neither be reaching for any special state nor straining to push away an unpleasant state just because it is unpleasant or difficult.

4.

Regardless of which practice you are drawn to or have the best aptitude for, it is important to cultivate the best skills with concentration that you can.

In this regard, it is important to discern if you are not attaining single point concentration because you may be trying to do so in an impatient and unskillful way, without doing the proper preparatory work. If the hindrance is that you have not done the preparatory work, then it makes sense to back-pedal and revisit the foundations of your practice before you try to add the upper stories to the house. If the hindrance is that you are just not working hard enough, then you have a decision to make. If you are reaching for advanced states of concentration as though they were another trophy to add to your shelf, or achievement to add to your resume, then appropriate adjustments of effort and intention also need to be made. But if, after careful and sustained efforts with competent teachers and suitably long and dedicated retreats, you simply are not attaining single point concentration, that is good information too. It seems you may not have this particular ability. If this is the case, then you simply utilize the skills with concentration you have developed. With these skills you can proceed to the further cultivation of the insights needed to diffuse internal hindrances and pierce any illusions that remain active.

On the other hand, if you are able to cultivate single point concentration, then it makes sense to proceed to the other advanced degrees of concentration which follow. In Buddhist practice these are referred to as the Jhana practices. In Greek and Russian Orthodox traditions, they are referred to as Pure Prayer or Prayer of the Heart. In the Catholic Discalced Carmelite tradition, they are referred to as the Prayer of Quiet and Prayer of Union. In Raja Yoga, they are referred to as Samadhi. Still, regardless of the spiritual context you are working in, if you have the aptitudes for such efforts or somehow these doors open widely for you, then it makes sense to walk through them. There are real benefits to doing so. *But it is important to remember that advanced states of concentration are still only preparatory skills.*

The final work is to cultivate the insight needed to diffuse whatever are the underlying causes and springing mechanisms that keep you bound in crude, unsatisfying, semi-unconscious states of grasping and aversion.

Remember the goal is not technical excellence with practice. The goal is great freedom and love. It is just that well-developed skills with technique make these goals more attainable.

What is important is that everyone has the same chance to attain this great freedom and this great love even if the road to these worthy experiences varies somewhat from one person to another.

5.

Whichever style of meditation you favor or are best suited for and whichever historical tradition you are drawn to, the work remains to be much the same. You will need to find healthy and creative ways to diffuse any fires of anger, guilt, fear, excessive desire, vanity, torpor, and illusion that are active in your life.

Towards that end the following practices are offered one chapter at a time:

- ▸ Affirmation and acceptance practice will help cool the fires of anger and aversion.

- ▸ Confession and the making of amends will extinguish the fires of guilt and shame.

- ▸ Cultivating better practical problem-solving skills will lead to a more stable life and thereby begin the work of diminishing fear.

- ▸ Reflections on faith and a vision of life you can freely accept will help diminish remaining levels of fear at depth. Such reflections and choices will also help dispel any nagging levels of doubt that may be present in a person's life as to whether liberation is even possible in this life.

- ▸ Humility will help cool and quiet the inflamed aspects of self and ego so that more subtle reflections on the true nature of the self and being can be engaged.

- ▸ The further cultivation of insight will help disperse any glaring illusions and delusions that may be active in one's life. From there a person can proceed also to diffuse the obvious and then the submerged and subtle illusions that distort their view and stunt their experience of life. From this sustained work, the fires and engines of excessive desire and any inflamed aspects of self and ego which are still active, will be further diminished.

An ancient Buddhist image is relevant in these efforts. In this simile our suffering is like a general fire that arises from many burning logs at night. As each log is pulled from the burning fire and doused with water, the overall heat and intensity of the fires of restlessness, dissatisfaction, and despair are lessened.

Over time all of the logs are scattered and doused with water. One can then lean over and look upon the burning embers and coals that make up the fire's pit. Then one can pour a large bucket of water on the burning embers and coals that remain.

When all the fires are extinguished the cool night air of liberation is what remains.

6.

Some of these practices such as affirmation, faith, and humility can be incorporated as themes of reflection during silent meditation sessions if one chooses to do so.

Some of these practices such as confession and the cultivation of practical skill are not engaged during meditation but rather are most effectively utilized during times of study and in the active hours of life.

You may wish to read through this entire work and then come back to certain practices you feel most drawn to. With careful discernment you will be able to develop your personal schedule or cycle of various meditations according to your own insights or in consultation with whomever you may be studying with.

Or you may wish to spend a week or a month or longer with any one practice before moving on to the next you feel drawn to.

Find the efforts that work best for you, but do not forego any practice just because it may be arduous.

While this is a simple path, it often is not an easy one.

7.

In general it is important to be aware that the typical suggestion of meditating twice a day for twenty or thirty minutes is a good beginning of practice. It is usually suggested these times occur before breakfast and before dinner when the abdomen is more light and clear. *This may be all the time most people have available until it becomes reasonably possible to simplify their life to free up more time for study practice.*

But, it is also important to be aware that a serious effort to develop single point concentration or the higher stages of insight practice will generally require greater commitments of time. While a great deal of progress can be made in the context of an ordinary life schedule, for a person to develop concentration and insight to a fine point will usually require longer commitments of time and disciplined effort. To reach the higher stages of the path, longer daily sittings and at least some dedicated retreats of a few weeks will be needed when you are reasonably able to make such commitments.

Cycles where one sits for half an hour and then walks mindfully for ten to fifteen minutes and then repeats this process over a period of two to three hours or longer, will also allow a person to settle into deeper states of peace and clarity.

If these kinds of time commitments seem daunting at first, don't be too concerned.

As you find it possible and desirable to make commitments to daily meditation practice, the energy and simplicity of life needed to sit for longer periods of time and longer retreats will arise sooner or later.

For those who wish to help this process along it is useful to note that one of the reasons monasteries and convents exist is to create an environment and a way of life where longer periods of sitting and deeper practice and searching can be done. Sadly, there are many regions of the world in our time where the monasteries and convents are in a protracted state of general decline. If this is also the case in your day and age, please don't be too discouraged. There will always be some people residing in the established houses who have persevered and developed good skills and exemplary witness. If you are patient, you can find such people and either find a way to enter such institutions as a member or receive spiritual direction from those people as a visiting lay person.

Should the doors of the established houses be closed to you for good or bad reasons, there are always some people with excellent skills who live at the margins of the official institutions and mainstream society. Perhaps you and they will be able to form the basis of a new monastery or convent. But if these connections do not arise then persevere on your own with the gentle awareness and knowledge that you will need to proceed at a realistic pace if there is not a lot in the way of available guidance and encouragement for serious effort.

The cycle of decline and renewal of monastic cultures has continued for at least a thousand years. It is unlikely it will end any time soon. The tendency of small groups of men and women to gather together in informal communities in remote places has continued for over two thousand years. It is equally unlikely this pattern of human behavior will end any time soon despite the coming upheavals to be caused by breakaway technological developments and overpopulation.

This is because there will always be people who need to and who want to go deeper. As simple groupings of such people are helpful for the cultivation of fellowship and skill and shared practice, there will always be a few who will choose this special way of common living and shared practice. There will always be a few who seek out these kinds of small but highly competent marginal groups even if they have to trudge through many a lonely forest or pass through many an urban ashram to find the right place and group.

8.

Some will choose to emphasize one or more of the following practices more than others.

Some will integrate these practices into their meditation sessions and the active hours of life in different ways than others will.

For example, many will find it helpful to begin each meditation session with affirmation practice as described in the next chapter as a way to calm the mind. After a few minutes, or perhaps longer, as their mind calms and clears, they may decide to shift their attention back to the basic practice of observing their breath and seeking to cultivate the steady awareness of single point concentration. Or they may decide to devote their entire session to extending their affirmation to offer love and kindness to all who live.

For another example, many may find their mind at times to be so jumpy it makes sense to engage the basics of insight practice and to notice whatever is arising in the moment. They may choose to scan the body to notice whatever sensations of the body are present or to focus on discerning whether the emotional state is satisfying, unsatisfying, or neutral. There may be some issue of the day they find they are mildly or strongly obsessing over which manifests as a repetitive word loop in their mind. They may decide it makes sense to simply observe this word loop as it keeps repeating and then finally passes and see what can be learned about all repetitive word loops by this process of observation.

After a few minutes or perhaps longer as the mind calms and clears, they may decide to shift their attention back to the basic practice of observing the sensations of their breath and to cultivating single point concentration. Or they may remain in an open supple state and continue to engage insight practice for the duration of their session.

For now it is enough to bear in mind that there are many advanced and refined practices of concentration, affirmation, and insight, and much more that could be written about each of them.

For now it is enough to keep it simple and find out what helps to calm and clear the mind and to develop a daily meditation practice.

It is enough to find what works best for you.

It is enough to find what helps to diminish suffering in your life and in the lives of others in the most creative ways possible.

If you encounter teachings that you do not understand or feel you cannot accept in good conscience then set them aside. You can come back to them at another time if you feel it makes sense to do so.

It is enough to discern which practices you do understand and freely accept which you know you could be making better efforts with.

It is enough then to make those better efforts as diligently as you reasonably can.

This is a good path. This is a true path. This is a simple path.

Affirmation

1.

Almost everyone knows that offering affirmation, love, and compassion more consistently towards their own life and to others is a foundational practice of any sincere spiritual path. For this reason it is all the more surprising that so few people make as careful and sustained an effort with this as they could.

This is unfortunate.

Affirmation is perhaps the best example of a practice that most people know they could be making better efforts with.

This practice of offering affirmation, love, forgiveness, and compassion more freely is another good example of a practice that can be engaged by anyone whether they believe in God or not.

There is another benefit to these practices that is even more subtle.

Learning to enhance the love and compassion you offer towards your own life and to all who live will generate increasingly deeper levels of experience and insight. These experiences and insights will be instrumental in helping a person progress to whatever is the next level of peace and understanding that is available to them.

Regardless of how clear or conflicted your present beliefs may be, all that is needed is to engage these practices with the highest degree of honesty, openness, and personal integrity you are capable of.

2.

With regard to the overall effort to diminish the underlying causes of stressful emotions and conflicted thoughts, these efforts of affirmation, love, forgiveness, and compassion will have many beneficial effects.

The ability to offer love and compassion towards your own life will help to diminish any feelings of self-reproach, feelings of worthlessness, and any feelings of inadequacy or inferiority that may be active in your life.

The ability to enhance the quality of love and respect you offer to those people in your life with whom healthy relations are a viable possibility will allow those relationships to be more sustaining for you. The joy, laughter, and fulfillment that arise from healthier relations will help diminish such feelings as loneliness, isolation, hopelessness, and alienation.

The ability to offer love and forgiveness towards those you are in conflict with, to the degree you are reasonably able to do so, will allow you to diminish such feelings as anger, resentment, harsh judgment, and any feelings of revenge and retribution you may be prone to.

To draw again upon the image that our suffering is like a fire that arises from a pile of many burning logs, these practices will remove quite a few of these burning logs.

While these changes will not happen overnight, they will happen and painful sources of stress and agitation in the mind will begin to be diffused.

Another benefit is that these efforts are additional ways to cultivate the clarity and continuity of awareness which, over time, will make concentration practice more attainable. The efforts to closely watch the arising of any feelings of anger, resentment, harsh judgment of others or low self-esteem, loneliness, alienation will help strengthen the ability to be more clearly aware of each moment.

As skills with mindful awareness become enhanced, they can be further engaged in this way:

> You can remember you have the ability to touch with conscious awareness and hold each emotional experience with patience and compassion for the suffering you have known or are currently experiencing.

Over time the strength and power of enhanced concentration will make another benefit possible. With patience and gentleness, as opposed to force and repression, you will learn how to make conscious choices to prevent unwholesome states from arising. Also, if such bitter feelings as angry resentment or low self-worth do arise, you can learn to skillfully mold and transform them into more wholesome and life-affirming states of mind.

Learning these skills of accepting, honoring, and then molding angry or resentful states into more wholesome states of mind creates a critical alternative to the destructive process of merely trying to repress aggressive urges.

3.

You can engage affirmation practice as a prelude of a few moments or minutes to any particular meditation session or as the theme of the entire session in a very simple way. After settling into a good and stable sitting posture, you can then make the clear and conscious effort to offer affirmation, love, and compassion towards your own life.

While in the beginning it might not be all that clear what it means to offer love and affirmation towards your own life, this question can be cleared up fairly quickly. One simple way is to offer your kindness by silently saying these words within, "May I be happy. May I be well. May I learn how to experience more peace and wisdom in my life." These simple phrases are enough to remind you of the positive wishes you have for yourself. These simple words will help call to mind brighter feelings than those which may have developed in the course of a busy and frustrating day.

Another way to offer this affirmation and care towards your own life is to call to mind the difficulties of your current life and the wounding experiences of the past that continue to be painful. Simply experiencing the suffering you have known and the distressed feelings you may be feeling in the present will be enough to stir feelings of compassionate care for your self. You can then silently offer this care and infuse your life experience with this care.

As you allow such experiences to surface, see if you can touch the experience of these feelings with awareness, patience, and compassion. This touching of any raw feelings and wounds with awareness and compassion will help heal any of the old or fresh wounds that may be active in your life.

It does need to be added that this is not done in some gushy or saccharine manner. Rather a simple tone of tenderness and kindness is all that is needed.

It is easy to forget how important it is to offer this silent gift of love and affirmation towards your own life and to skip this effort and focus instead on the breath or offering compassion towards others or some other aspect of practice.

To forego this step would be unfortunate as the efforts to heal the wounded self and ego precede the ability to begin to explore the true nature of the self and ego.

To forego this step would mean the ability to offer love to others would remain impaired.

4.

Another positive way to engage this practice is to silently offer forgiveness to yourself for any poor or terrible choices that made your life and the lives of others more difficult.

Part of this effort is to understand at a visceral level that decisions made long ago cannot be changed and that strong feelings of regret, or futile anguish over "what might have been" only add to the stresses of the present. Even though almost everyone knows the past cannot be changed, many still have a hard time forgiving themselves. They keep rehashing critical moments and choices in the past and wishing with a completely futile hunger they had done things differently.

This is another good example of a very basic practice which almost everyone understands but still tends not to do.

Until you genuinely forgive yourself and let go of regrets, there will never really be enough peace or insight to understand the value of forgiving others or the strength to actually follow through on this intention.

None of this is meant to imply that this work is easy or quick.

If you have let yourself down by poor or just plain terrible choices in the past, it may be hard to forgive yourself or let go of regrets. This is especially true if those choices generated difficult, long-term consequences in the present that are very hard to cope with. A prolonged struggle with genuine hardship in your present day-to-day life, caused in large part by poor or terrible choices in the past, can trigger frequent feelings of regret and self-reproach in the present unless one is quite vigilant.

Furthermore, you may well make new mistakes or poor choices that generate additional consequences that are hard to bear and so forgiveness of self needs to be ongoing.

What is important to realize is that learning how to genuinely forgive yourself and then actually doing this work is more than just a nice sounding spiritual idea. This work is an essential part of the process to free up the energy needed to work through present problems. You may definitely need to seek the forgiveness of others to complete this process of healing and reconciliation, but the process needs to start with offering love and forgiveness towards yourself.

You can extend this practice during meditation and in the active hours of life in this way:

> See if you can notice every shade of regret, self-reproach, low self-worth, or general feelings of inadequacy if any such feelings arise within you. See if you can remember to touch these old reflexive feelings with a conscious effort to be more patient, compassionate, and gentle with yourself.

See how your experience of the images you have of yourself and your experience of life begin to shift as you become skilled in this effort. It is likely you will find such efforts very much like watering a plant that has begun to droop and wither.

There may be people in your life who do undermine your confidence in overt or covert ways.

It is important to make sure you are not one of them.

If others are clearly not on your side it is all the more important to have the presence of mind to bolster your own sense of strength and confidence. It is important, in a figurative way, to stand by yourself as a strong and confident defender and ally.

It is important to offer real compassion towards your own life for the suffering you have known, forgiveness for the mistakes you have made, and to cultivate a general optimism with regards to the joy and freedom you wish to know.

During these efforts you can either maintain a parallel awareness on the breath if you wish to or let go of the awareness of the breath in favor of committing all your awareness to these sustained efforts of affirmation.

5.

After a few moments or minutes of offering such forgiveness and affirmations towards your own life, you can extend this general intention in this way. As you continue to sit still and breathe, you can call to mind those people whom you love the most and with whom you have the least conflict. You can offer your silent gift of compassion to them during your meditation for their life and for the hopes they have for love and freedom. This offering can be as simple as this:

> "May they be happy. May they be well." "May they and their families know the joy and prosperity that all families seek."

You can proceed after a while to call to mind those people whom you like but perhaps do not love, if for no other reason than you don't know them that well.

> "May they be happy. May they be well." "May they and their family know the peace and love that all families seek."

You can proceed after a while to call to mind those people whom you know but do not have feelings for much one way or another.

> "May they be happy. May they be well." "May they and their family know the peace and love that all families seek."

Don't be fooled by whatever cold or indifferent or arrogant exterior other people may have. Whether they know it or not everyone wants and needs to be loved. Everyone at some point experiences loneliness and fears the possibility of unexpected reverses, poverty, illness, unfulfillment or betrayal in love, devastating loss, old age, and death. Once you gain the ability to peer through the mask of those who appear to be cold and indifferent, you will see they too fear loss, suffering, and death in pretty much the same ways that you do.

This realization that they know the same general and at times intense suffering as you have known will further stir nascent capacities of compassionate sympathy. As you stir up these feelings of compassion within you and offer that compassion more regularly towards others, this will change the experience of your life and your experience of others. It will become easier and more natural to offer simple positive intentions.

"May they be happy. May they be well." "May they and their family know the peace and love that all families seek."

"May they find the love in their marriage that they hoped to find when they were young."

"May they find a way to lower crime and increase justice and stability in their town."

"May they find a way to increase jobs and opportunities for the people of their town."

"May they be healthy and strong."

6.

For those who do believe in God, or are moved to explore the possibility that God does exist, you can extend this intention of silent, compassionate giving in this additional way:

You can call to mind the image of God that you feel is most true, or some great saint whose example you value greatly. When you have turned your thoughts towards your chosen subject you can offer the gift of your love and appreciation to God or whoever it is you feel drawn to venerate in this way.

You can say silently within yourself as though you were kneeling alone in some gray stone chapel at midnight:

"I love you O God of heaven and earth."

Or to some departed saint or living exemplar:

"I love you and thank you for your witness and sacrifice."

You can fuse your love, awareness, and intention and concentrated effort into a pure and steady devotional adoration. With such efforts you can blend the practice of affirmation with uninterrupted, concentrated effort.

You may wish to maintain your focus on the breath and add this act of veneration as a second focus. Or, you can let go of the focus on the breath and shift all of your concentrated awareness to this act of silent giving.

Loving God can be your chosen theme for single point concentration.

In either preference you can center on the silent offering of your love directly to the sacred heart of the God of heaven and earth.

You can become a living stream of devotion: radiant, transfigured, and free.

7.

If you do not believe in God you can still offer such sentiments of devotion to some revered meditation teacher or mentor.

"I love you and thank you for your life and example."

Or you can call to mind each of the members of your sangha or meditation community and offer this simple benevolent intention:

"May you find the liberation and profound peace you seek."

8.

At some point in a particular session of meditation on the breath and affirmation you can make the decision to extend this practice in any one of a number of ways.

For example: as you realize you have drifted off in yet another distraction, you can pause to consider who you were thinking of during the distraction whether it was yourself or some friend or nemesis. In this way you can use the content of the distraction to further cultivate affirmation, by offering a fresh stream of positive silent love towards yourself or whomever you were thinking about during the distraction.

For another example you can offer love and compassion to every name you read in the daily newspaper without conditions and without measuring whether they deserve such love or not.

For another example you can offer love and compassion to every person who is present as different memories come to mind, and by infusing memories with compassion, begin to transform the vast warehouses of memory.

If you are reading history you can offer compassion to yourself for the experiences of suffering you feel when reading of past tragedies and to every name in history you happen to read about.

If you are reading scripture you can offer compassion to every name and being profiled in the scriptures of your chosen path.

In these ways, and others you may think of, you can further expand the practice of offering silent affirmation to all who live, to all who ever have lived, and all who ever will live.

Or, if you do not wish to further expand this practice of affirmation as you proceed deeper into a meditation session, that is fine as well.

You can quietly let go of these intentions of affirmation and silent offering and simply shift your intention and awareness back to sensations of the breath in the nostrils. You can migrate back to the more narrow effort of cultivating the pure and wordless focus of single point concentration or your insight practice.

Either choice is a good one.

In either case the work needs to continue to reflect upon any anger, resentment, harsh judgment, aggressive urges, or actions if any such feelings arise during silent meditation or in the active hours of life. It is important to know it will not be possible to quiet the mind or cultivate any real degree of concentration or love until you find healthy ways to diminish at depth any such feelings that may be active in your life.

It will also not be possible to quiet the mind or cultivate any real degree of concentration or love until you find healthy ways to diminish any feelings of low self-esteem or feelings of inadequacy or superiority that may be active in your life.

It will also not be possible to quiet the mind unless you learn to diminish any general feelings of loneliness, isolation, and alienation that may arise from not properly tending to the primary relations in your life with as much kindness, consideration, and integrity as possible.

The good news is that your choice to improve the quality of affirmation and love you have to offer your own life and others is a great beginning to help attain all these important benefits.

9.

Some may prefer to do the work of looking into any experiences of anger, resentment, harsh judgment, aggressive urges or actions as part of their personal study or journaling. Some may feel the need or desire to do so by working with a counselor experienced with anger management and helping people with general issues they have with love and respect.

The choice is up to you. What is important is to find a way that works.

What is important is that you begin to think carefully about who you do love and seek to improve the quality of love and respect you offer to them one day, one encounter at a time.

There is a very simple way to engage this effort. Every time you meet someone new or someone you know you can ask yourself, "What am I offering to the silent empty space between me and this person? Is it judgment or am I offering a simple, natural respect and courtesy?"

If the answer is the former, see what you can do to shift to the latter. If the answer is the latter then see what you can do to be ever more natural and sincere in this respect.

As you stir up your natural inclinations and abilities to love, this will help enhance the most important relations in your life. This will lead to greater sustaining fulfillment in those relations.

It is in this way that the effort to offer love to others will help diminish any feelings of loneliness, isolation, and alienation that may be active in your life.

The effort to more instinctively and naturally offer regard and respect to all you encounter will also tend to improve work and community relations. As this happens life will become, by degree, more stable and enjoyable. These enhancements will also help calm and clear the mind during meditation and in the experiences and choices of daily life.

These changes will also support the refinement of intuitive and practical problem-solving skills and so there is yet another benefit to the simple choice to value love more highly and to offer love more naturally.

10.

What is also important is to begin to think about who you do not love or who you may really despise or hate with a burning passion.

There is no need to offer love and kindness towards the people whom you really dislike, at least not yet. The day will come when you will want to find whatever help and guidance you can from others and from your own inner resources to learn how to love and forgive those people who by all ordinary reckoning deserve no such consideration. That day does not have to be today or tomorrow, but someday. While it is true that hopefully that day will come sooner rather than later, it is also true that people with high degrees of anger and harsh judgment will need to work with such feelings at a realistic pace.

As you begin, it is enough to at least be willing to someday try to learn to forgive even grievous wrongs if that is as much as you can do to start.

As motivation for this willingness, it is enough to know that learning someday to proactively silently offer affirmation and love to all beings is necessary for liberation. The ability to sit in meditation and silently offer this gift to all beings with a free and radiant heart, and to also do so in at least some of the ordinary moments of your active life, is one of the signs you are well on your way.

But if others have badly hurt you or those you love or are threatening to do so, or are doing so in the present, it is understandable there may be little in the way of love in your heart for them.

It may take many a long century before anyone understands why so many in this world have to be so petty, or outright violent, exploitative, and cruel. For now it is enough to love those you love the most and to offer this affirmation towards your own life as well.

Someday you can do a little more, and then a little more than that.

This act of choosing love, the best love you have to offer, will transform your life.

You will be able to forgive more and more of the petty offenses others have inflicted upon you and someday you can proceed to cast your affirmations and intentions to those who are truly wicked and evil.

As you become more and more skilled at love, many of your most serious doubts or unanswered questions will fade from view.

The purifications needed to actively offer love to all beings in silent meditation and to do so as a central theme of one's life will awaken transforming experiences and consolation.

It is simple.

We are transformed by love.

11.

Regrettably, many commentaries on unconditional love seem to imply that a few meditation sessions are enough to tame truly violent and conflicted impulses. For many people this is not the case. Anger and even impotent rage can be such deeply habitualized responses for many that diffusing the underlying causes of such feelings will probably be long-term work.

There is also no need to imagine you will no longer experience surges of anger and frustration just because you have begun to make some high-grade commitments to love and affirmation. It will take most people quite a while to really learn how to diffuse at depth the underlying causes of anger, resentment, harsh judgment, or aggression.

If there are high levels of various forms of anger and resentment active in your life it is important to find and then to feel the feelings that are there. It is important to find someone you can really talk to about any such deep feelings or aggressive thoughts and urges especially if your thoughts and urges are raw, vivid, and vicious.

Any efforts to repress or deny such feelings will only create significant levels of stress and cause very real damage to your psyche and bodily health. In addition to this damage, there is another general problem that arises. The repression of anger doesn't work. It just creates a pressure cooker in the mind causing the mind to erupt in even more vitriolic outbursts of rage and aggression if certain conditions come together as triggers to such a reaction.

This is especially true if you have been the victim of childhood abuse or neglect or some violent crime such as rape, a humiliating public beating, raw exploitation, or political repression.

If this is the case in your life, then even greater care and patience will be needed to find the right care-givers and teachers to work with.

If you can't quite find the right person to talk with, then keep searching but get what help you can if you feel it is getting harder to control aggressively violent urges.

You will know the right person in this way:

> They will not judge you for your anger or your rage. Nor will they offer cheap advice or platitudes about how you should be willing to love or pray for those who have hurt you badly *before you are really able or willing to do so.*

A mature mentor will honor and respect your feelings and encourage you to do the same.

They will also help make sure you know that it is one thing to feel serious levels of anger but that it is necessary to learn how to restrain any thoughts of retribution or unjustifiable militant action you may have a raw aching hunger to do.

12.

There is more that needs to be said about those rare situations when one needs to defend themselves against true criminals, predators, and dictators. In truth there may be times when you personally or your society may not see any other way to defend yourself or your nation from organized gangsters or predatory sadists or genuinely ruthless dictators or their henchmen. If such deeply disturbing situations develop in your life or society, then people may understandably feel there is no legitimate option but to turn to militant means to protect and defend the vulnerable. Surely this is a clear violation of the tenets of unconditional love and forgiveness. Still, if after careful review according to disciplined criteria you feel militant action is the only way to defend your life or the lives of others, then proceed with decisive action. But, proceed only with the clear intent to cause as little suffering as is needed to restrain or destroy the aggressors and to return to peaceful means as quickly as possible. Any sense of enjoyment of the suffering inflicted on others is a clear sign you have lost your way and been swept up in primitive emotions. Such atavistic emotions will have long-term destructive consequence for you if you do not revert back to a sense of lamentation that no other way besides militant action seemed to be available.

The trouble is that most of us, and most nations, reach for the militant option much too quickly even though other available and possibly effective remedies have not been exhausted. It is easy for even good and sensible people in mass cultures to be swept away by the fear and anger whipped up by cynical demagogues in ways that can lead to terrible wars and devastation that simply never needed to happen.

For now it is enough to make sure you are doing what you can to diminish the anger, fear, and excessive desire in your life which are the little drops of poison that fill the buckets that spill over into war.

If you are able to remain true to the highest standards of non-violence and are willing to die or be imprisoned for your beliefs then more power to you, for this is a very high practice.

But for most of us what is realistically possible is to commit to developing whatever is the next level of non-violent conflict resolution skills one is capable of and to reserve acts of violence when such are truly the last resort to defend the innocent.

Real commitments to steady incremental progress in one's life and society along these lines will allow for real progress towards a non-violent world.

This is a good hope. This is a true hope. This is a simple hope.

Confession and Grace

1.

It is not as though the early efforts with affirmation and love will diminish all anger at depth and then you proceed to do the same with guilt and shame.

The process of calming and clearing the mind is not that programmatic.

It is more that one diminishes the most glaring forms of anger and resentment and then proceeds to work on the most pronounced experiences of guilt and shame. After working on these efforts, one can proceed to diminish any vivid experiences of fear, excessive desire, and vanity. From there one can labor to further diminish any experiences of torpor and illusion that may still be active in their life. Month by month, year by year, decade by decade, one continues to lower by degree the overall fire and heat of passionate feelings, serious doubts, excessive desires, and deluded thoughts.

Month by month, year by year, decade by decade, more of the burning logs will have been removed from the bonfires of suffering and doused with buckets of clear, cool water. Once the burning logs have been removed and extinguished, it will be possible to pour water on the burning embers and coals in the fire's pit and scatter the ashes.

It is the steadiness and sincerity of effort, and the cumulative benefit of how each of these practices complement one another, which leads to increasingly refined levels of peace, wisdom, insight, and understanding.

2.

These practices of confession, remorse, and atonement are offered to dispel any feelings of guilt and shame that may be active in your life. They too can be engaged whether a person does or does not believe in God, although the form of this practice will vary according to beliefs.

As this happens, your mind will further calm and clear.

Diminishing guilt will also help diffuse repressed anger and resentment as anger and resentments are common travelling companions to the pangs of guilt and shame that have not been tended to.

As mentioned in the opening sections of affirmation practice, forgiving yourself for poor choices is a good beginning to diminish regret and self-reproach. Admitting genuine faults, seeking the forgiveness of others, where such forgiveness can be found, feeling remorse for the pain you have caused, and atoning for negative behaviors and actions where that is reasonably possible, will generate additional relief.

Another critical benefit is that these efforts will also free up important types of energy needed to resolve the pressing problems of your current life.

Whether others accept your offer of apology and atonement or not is not your issue. It is their issue.

What is important is the thoroughness and sincerity of your confession and remorse and your meaningful efforts to change negative behaviors, attitudes, and ways of speaking. In this practice, sincerity and thoroughness are all that is needed, and all that will work.

If there is any one practice with which you want to make sure you do not make poor efforts, it is this one.

Whatever name you choose to call the reservoirs of energy within you that arise from acts of confession, remorse, and atonement is up to you. What is important is that anyone who sincerely engages these practices will find this very special energy arising within them as a result of making meaningful changes in the ways they treat others.

Christians call this energy grace.

Christians believe this grace is essential to the process of transforming a person's inner character and will and resolving conflicts at depth within people and between people. This practice and the awareness of the centrality of grace is one of the cardinal contributions Christians have made to the world. None of this is to imply that a person needs to become a Christian to engage this practice of opening to grace. There may be other aspects of standard Christian dogma many feel they cannot in good conscience accept. But exploring how the subtle and positive energy that arises from confession of wrongs committed can transform character and volition is a practice that can be adopted by anyone.

If you prefer a different name than grace for this special quality of healing energy in the mind, then find or develop some different term. But, regardless of the words you choose, the suggestion is given that you take the time to explore the truth and reality of grace by sincere and thorough examinations of conscience and acts of confession and atonement as needed. What is also suggested is that you learn to be aware of and to work with this special form of energy as skillfully and openly as possible.

3.

There is one primary reason why many people do not ever reach the levels of spiritual insight and experience that are available to them. This is because many are simply unwilling to admit openly and freely any actions, words, negative attitudes, or opinions that cause harm to others. Neither are many willing to make the best efforts they reasonably can to make meaningful change in the ways they treat others so that they do not cause new offense. This is the tragedy of individuals, nations, business entities, non-profit organizations, community groups, municipal councils, churches, monasteries, and civilizations.

If more people, if the majority of people, if the vast majority of people, were willing to engage this simple, but sometimes unsettling effort, then this world would be a very different place.

The tragedy is that this effort needs no money or new governmental budgets or institutional rescues across global borders.

All that is needed is an understanding that everything changes within individuals when they become very honest with themselves. Everything changes when a person becomes completely honest about any of their actions, words, attitudes, or opinions that have inflicted pain on others.

For those who see the general trends of towns, nations, religions, and mass cultures, and who perceive the need for new kinds of leaders and servants, this is the practice that opens all doors.

If you are stubborn, insensitive, rigid, selfish, crude, cheap, or downright cold or vicious, then admit it to yourself and then to whomever you trust the most for guidance and support.

What is the spiritual path?

It is a path of becoming more open to see who you really are in both your best and most anti-social qualities, however submerged, or hidden from your awareness, those anti-social drives may be. A spiritual practice honestly engaged is a willingness to see all aspects of who you are as compared with who you think you are or pretend to be on Sunday mornings or church suppers.

It is a path of becoming more honest and open to real change at the depths of your being.

This practice is not about some superficial rearranging of furniture, or learning to recite beautiful passages of scripture from memory while continuing to brandish your switchblades in secret.

This practice is about real change at depth in the way you offer love and respect to all with whom you are in relationship, which is to say with all who live.

Finally committing to loving those whom you say you love: this is the spiritual path.

Finally following through with sincere humility to become a more decent human being.

This is a good way. This is a true way. This is a simple way.

4.

Many experiences of guilt, shame, and embarrassment are excessive and need to be seen as being excessive and then tended to in a reasonable and mature way.

Many other experiences of guilt, shame, and embarrassment are justifiable reactions to the disgraceful ways a person has treated others. These feelings need to be ameliorated by healthy means and strong, conscious effort for a very simple reason.

Guilt, shame, and embarrassment are additional layers and clusters of stress and agitation that prevent a deeper relationship with one's own life and with all of life. Guilt, shame, and embarrassment are additional layers and clusters of stress and agitation *that prevent the best skills with concentration and insight from developing.* They need to be diffused at depth. The only way to do that is to speak openly and freely within yourself and with those whom you trust the most about any negative tendencies, behaviors, or any dirty little secrets of your life and heart. The next step is to follow through with a sincere willingness to change your ways for the better.

Clearly seeing and admitting to negative streaks within your behaviors and attitudes is one level of confrontation with your life and the truth.

Speaking openly to another person and freely admitting any cheap, grossly selfish, or evil choices you have made is another even deeper level of confrontation with yourself and with the truth.

Approaching those you need to make amends to and offering genuine apologies and commitments to real change in the relationship and offering to be accountable for that commitment to change is a still deeper level of confrontation. At every stage of this confrontation and admission, the false self, the puffed up, inflamed, the mildly or substantially dishonest aspects of who you are, are deflated. This deflation allows for the deeper and more creative energies of the psyche and soul to surface throughout all the layers of self.

It is these more creative and more pure energies, which are often called grace, that many feel are the only forces capable of transforming the will, the mind, and the heart into something noble, fine, and beautiful.

The reality, nature, and efficacy of this energy or grace is consistently missed by many depth psychologists, yet it is this grace that can reform the violently conflicted self and heart. If you believe in God, then your practice of confession, remorse, atonement, and reconciliation will take one general shape, although the particular form of confession will vary depending on the religious culture you are committed to.

If you do not believe in God, then your practice of this general effort will be to admit your faults in the context of your tradition and to honor your commitments to become the most ethical and decent person you possibly can be.

For people following either way of confession, what needs to happen is to follow through and make the changes needed in your life to match the high standards of personal integrity and conscious living you have embraced.

For people following either way of confession, high standards of personal integrity, decency, and a willingness to make the changes needed to live up to those standards are essential. It is simple. You need to be willing to work through any and all tendencies of hypocrisy in your life. Regardless of which way of life you follow or which view of truth you are committed to, please do not underestimate the importance of giving this practice your very best efforts throughout the course of your entire life.

If you find yourself unwilling for any reason to engage this practice with a full heart and as clear a determination as you are reasonably capable of, then you would be right to be very concerned.

Confession, remorse, and atonement are the most essential practices of the path of liberation.

You will make no real progress without them.

If you look closely at the catastrophes of nations and religions, you will see these calamities arise from a common source: poor individual efforts with this practice multiplied on a large scale.

When you encounter weak, indifferent, or downright hypocritical priests, ministers, or other spiritual teachers, you can rightly assume the weakness or failure of their witness arises because they have neglected this elemental practice. Regardless of how much time ministers, priests, counselors, or teachers spend in classrooms studying the rules, customs, and thick books of their faith and creed, without this practice they are not honoring the call they feel they have heard.

Please, please do not become a dull functionary or mediocre representative of your faith.

The good news is that all you need to do to avoid that gray fate is to be true to that practice of confession and reconciliation you feel is rigorous and true without making the other mistake of drifting into some morbid form of scrupulosity.

Genuine confession and reconciliation allow grace to emerge into personal consciousness.

Grace generates life, transformation, and creativity.

Fear and Practical Skills

1.

As part of their effort to work through their confusion about what to believe, many people expend significant efforts to study complex theological doctrines and questions such as transubstantiation or codependent origination.

At times, and with a good process, there can be genuine benefit to doing so. But it is not beneficial if one is straining to find answers or is stuck in anguished confusion about how to decide between what different forceful teachers assert are the truths of such subjects.

There is other work that can be done and other approaches that can be considered.

You can turn and more clearly face whatever may be the genuine challenges of your life and any important decisions that need to be made.

You can take the time to learn better practical problem-solving skills. This will help you respond more effectively to any difficult conditions that may be active in your life.

As practical steps are taken to more effectively respond to genuine challenges and opportunities, this will help diminish fear, anxiety, and any feelings of inadequacy that may be active in your life. As you become more successful at solving problems and making the best use of opportunities, your life will become more stable. All of this will give rise to a greater sense of confidence in your sense of personal worth and health.

Your mind and heart will further calm and clear. Concentration will deepen. More refined insights will arise.

2.

The earlier practices of affirmation and confession will begin to cool the fires of anger and guilt. Better practical problem-solving skills will support these efforts and also begin the process of cooling the fires of fear. Quieting the fires of fear will then make it more possible to resolve doubts. Resolving doubt in turn will give rise to a stronger general sense of confidence and more consistent efforts with meditation practice. All of this will help diffuse fear at deeper levels.

A beneficial cycle will have been set in motion.

But, as helpful as better practical problem-solving skills will be, it will also be necessary to explore other ways to diminish doubt so that the deeper work with fear is possible. Towards this end the following chapter on "Fear and Faith" offers additional ways to help diminish both fear and doubt at deeper levels. In the following chapter, suggestions are offered to help a person think about faith and to consider how they can find a vision of life and faith they can freely accept and make real commitments to.

The general tone of the next chapter is not to suggest that you have faith in this or that doctrine or religion unless you freely choose to do so.

Rather suggestions are offered to help support your search for a vision of life and truth that clearly and naturally makes sense to you. The general process is to find healthy and clear ways to resolve doubt so a person will naturally feel motivated to make stronger commitments to the values and specific practices of meditation they feel are best.

Still, it is understood that discerning a vision of life that one can have faith in may not be the easiest thing to do.

Just taking the time to understand what basic vision of life you do have is a good place to start.

Just realizing that the vision of life you have may be a bit cloudy or not that well thought out, or that you have serious conflicts with the vision of life you were taught earlier in life will be helpful.

What do you believe is the truth of this life?

Is it possible there really is nothing that you actually have faith in besides death and taxes?

Is it possible to find a vision of life you can freely accept and have faith in?

3.

The basic premise of both this chapter and the next is that finding healthy ways to diminish fear at depth is essential for many reasons.

First, diminishing fear also supports the diminishing of anger at depth. This is because fear is always a major driver and baseline element of anger and aggression. After all, if you are not afraid of losing something, why would you care enough to get angry one way or the other?

Second, diminishing fear will also allow you to face any pangs of guilt and shame you may have been dodging. Once you realize that confession and atonement provide credible ways to absolve any justifiable experiences of guilt and shame you have not dealt with, there will be less fear and trepidation about facing up to some unpleasant truths of your life. It will also be more possible to go through what may be an awkward process of making those amends that need to be made.

Third, diminishing fear will also diminish excessive desire. A great deal of excessive desire arises as a way to hide from, or to escape from, the various fears and anxieties one may have which they have not been willing to face.

Fourth, diminishing fear will also help you to take greater risks with the search for love and intimacy. You will come to realize you no longer need to be as afraid of rejection or abandonment by those who may be willing to commit their affections to you. As a person becomes more secure, they realize that rejection, abandonment, and loss still may happen but they are no longer as afraid of such risks and prospects as they might have been. Imbued with a greater sense of confidence, resiliency, and fortitude, a person knows they can bear such reverses should they arise. Previously their fears and apprehensions might have been strong enough to keep them from taking any risks at all with other people. Now they can enter fully into life and take the risks with love and meeting new friends that others have successfully taken. This is a major benefit.

Fifth, a detailed study of the fears one has is another excellent way to further cultivate mindful awareness. As always, a steady enhancement of your skills with mindful awareness will support the long-term efforts to cultivate the best quality skills with concentration and insight needed for the deeper experiences of peace and clarity to arise.

In the deeper experiences of peace, consciousness is enhanced. These enhancements to consciousness and the perceptual faculties are uniquely beneficial. As a person emerges from these deep states of peace, they will find they can reflect more skillfully upon those remaining doubts and unanswered questions they feel they have a fair chance of resolving.

Sixth, as fear is diminished at depth this will clear the way to more creatively face and respond to remaining painful situations of your life that could not be tended to earlier. As fear is diminished you will also be able to enjoy more fully those experiences of joy and well-being that arise.

4.

Understandably, if there are very real problems in your life which need to be resolved, these situations may give rise to strong feelings of fear and anxiety. Such feelings are normal and useful alarm bells that draw one's attention to a genuine problem, or threat. Learning how to develop more skillful responses to difficult situations is an important part of the spiritual path and the general efforts to diminish justifiable fears and anxieties.

But it is equally important to learn through mindful observation how to spot the difference between justifiable experiences of fear and old patterns of excessive anxiety that are out of proportion to whatever situations are present. A clear understanding when one is caught up in excessive anxiety and worry creates the opportunity to diffuse these old habit patterns once and for all.

None of this is to imply that this may be easy to do. Difficult situations which kick up justifiable fear are by definition hard to resolve.

Overcoming the inertia of old habits of excessive anxiety also usually requires real effort over a sustained period of time. *But however difficult or favorable your life conditions may be, better practical problem-solving skills added to the practices already offered will help with all of this.*

Resolving long-standing problems will also free up quality time and energy for other pursuits. In fact, the surges of energy that surface when you experience real triumphs over difficult and long standing problems is another very interesting field of observation and practice of mindful awareness.

Usually, though, it may take a while to see any noticeable changes in your life. But over time you will see that you are successfully enhancing the peace, simplicity, and stability of your life.

There will be more time and better quality time for those personal and work relations that are important to you.

There will be more time for you.

There will be more time and better quality time for study and silent meditation practice. The more time you have for silent meditation, the more deeply you will be able to further your skills with all of the related practices needed to cultivate awareness and concentration and insight.

Deeper concentration and richer insights will, in turn, further support ongoing improvements with practical problem-solving and a virtuous cycle will have been set in motion.

5.

Before proceeding, it needs to be acknowledged that quite a bit of this work will be much more difficult for anyone who is suffering from mild or acute anxiety disorders or paranoia. This is because their fears are being generated by trauma and/or malfunctioning biochemistry in their brain rather than from more typical causes and threats in everyday life.

The work to diminish fear may also be much more difficult for those in early stages of recovery from violent attack, raw political repression, or some other equally difficult set of life conditions.

Those who have experienced the raw violence of this life rightly suspect there is no real reason their bad experiences could not happen again, although hopefully they will not. For such people, diffusing and letting go of fear will be more difficult. The silver lining for people who have known such deeply disturbing experiences is that their efforts will be all the more beneficial when they finally do learn how to diminish fear at depth.

Still, special care needs to be taken by anyone who is in the early stages of recovery from severe trauma such as childhood abuse, rape, war, or other forms of physical and emotional violence. It is all the more important for such people to proceed with greater care as they turn to more clearly face their fears and traumatic experiences. It is all the more important they do so only when they feel ready to do so, and then only in a safe setting with very experienced guides.

Still, these basic reflections on fear, practical skills, and faith will be good supports to the general recovery of people afflicted with anxiety disorders as well. The same holds true for those recovering from addiction or violent trauma even if the progress of recovery may be slower and more difficult.

6.

The first practical problem-solving skill is to learn how to openly face and name your fears.

Compiling a list of your fears will prove to be instructive and a real relief.

As the suggestion was made in the previous chapter to write out a list of all angers and resentments, *the suggestion is now made to write out a similar list of your fears.* When you are ready, when you are able, take the time to articulate all the fears you are aware of. Look also for any feelings of dread or nagging anxieties that you vaguely know are there but which you tend not to admit to yourself, let alone to anyone else.

But before you do this, it can be helpful to employ a clever trick in your efforts to openly face and name one's fears.

This trick is to realize it is enough to simply face and name the fears without immediately jumping into wondering how you can possibly resolve the troubles from which the fears arise.

The work of taking action will come soon enough but it does not need to happen right away unless there is some emergency or you are simply ready to roll up your sleeves and get started.

In the beginning it is enough to simply face the fears and openly name them out loud to yourself and to one other mature person, should you happen to know such a person.

This actually is a big step.

Take the time to pause as you name your fears. See if you can refrain from immediately jumping in and straining to try and figure out what you might be able to do about the underlying problem or threat. Without wondering right away what actions to consider, simply admit in detail which fears or anxieties are present within you and speak openly about these concerns to whomever it is you trust the most with such personal information. If you don't know anyone who is particularly skillful or trustworthy, then you may need to write out your concerns and your thoughts about what you need to do and then keep your own counsel. But usually there is someone in the family, the professional care-giving community, the clergy, or a well-regarded meditation teacher who will be able to offer at least general support. Hopefully you will be able to find someone fairly quickly who is the right choice to help you with the journey you are on.

However, there are quite a few people presenting themselves as guides or teachers whose skills and integrity are not well formed. It is simple. You need to be judicious about whom you do decide to confide in.

You can tell who is and who is not a mature counselor in this way:

> A mature counselor or guide will not jump in with quick solutions or advice but will honor both you and the fears you have as valuable experiences you can work with. They will simply receive you and your concerns without emotionally-charged judgments or a dismissive attitude.

An experienced guide will also wait until asked for their opinion or advice or they will ask for permission to give advice or opinions before doing so.

For those who are recovering from violent trauma, it is helpful to repeat this general cautionary note. You may well need to proceed slowly with this effort and then only with a very experienced guide and in a setting that you feel is really very safe for you. Please know that if this is the case with you, you are not alone. Best wishes are offered for your ongoing recovery.

7.

Once you write out a list of your fears, you can then compare it with your anger list.

From this you will begin to see more clearly the point-by-point correlation between specific incidents of anger and specific incidents of fear.

Also, as you learn to look carefully at the nature of various distractions that come up during meditation, you will see how many arise directly or indirectly from undercurrents of fear and worry.

It will become ever clearer how important it is to diminish all the various shades of fear such as worry, anxiety, insecurity, dread, as well as any feelings of inferiority and inadequacy that may be active in your life.

Still the questions abound as to what are the best ways to diminish fear at the most primal levels. Those who believe in God will tend to answer these questions in different ways than those who do not believe in God. Whichever of these basic descriptions most accurately describe your views, the following practical problem-solving techniques will help get the process started.

These simple efforts will help diminish both excessive and justifiable fears.

These skills will enhance the stability of your life. There will be more quality time for meditation and practice and other important pursuits.

As the mind clears and becomes more calm you will be better able to discern the ways that seem most true to you to diminish fear at more elemental levels.

The questions of faith, fear, doubt, and belief posed in the next chapter may be quite a bit more difficult for some to resolve one way or the other. That is all right. Just keep working with those practices you do feel you understand well. Just keep working with those teachings you either freely accept or are at least willing to freely explore.

Still, regardless of what conclusions you may come to as a result of reflecting on the questions and ideas in the next chapter, they remain to be important subjects to work with.

What vision of life do you believe in?

Do you have any good basic working decision of what the word faith means?

If you do have faith in the teachings of a particular tradition, how can this faith help you further diminish fear and doubt?

How does your faith help to awaken deeper experiences of love, peace, wisdom, and sacred beauty?

How does your faith help you to love more freely and vulnerably?

8.

A second practical problem-solving skill is to determine if an experience of fear or worry is an excessive reaction to problems that are minor in nature or a justified reaction that any healthy person would have to a genuine problem or serious threat.

In this effort your developing skills of awareness and concentration will be of real help.

These skills will help you to look and see more clearly and in greater detail both the experiences and causes of fear as well as the most skillful means to diminish fear.

Look carefully as whispers or storms of fear, anxiety, worry, dread, or feelings of inferiority or inadequacy arise. See if the feelings of fear and worry arise from speculations about future possible situations that really may not happen or that would not be that significant even if they did happen. Remember to come back to the moment when you realize the mind has wandered off into some fear-based scenario.

Come back to the present and touch your feet to the floor or ground as a way of remembering that you are in the present and not in some fear-based speculative scenarios about future events. Pinch yourself on the arm if you need to focus your awareness away from some unknown future scenario back to the reality of the present moment.

Look closely at the arising of any fears, anxieties, worries, insecurities, or feelings of inadequacy as they arise within. Try to notice how any such feelings impact your body, your mind, and your process of making sound decisions.

Try to observe in greater detail the changes in the body, breath, and mind as fear or worry creeps or surges in.

Try to catch the arising of fear when it is a small fire.

See if you can pour a bucket of water on small fires before they grow into larger conflagrations. If you can't, that will have to be all right as well. Try at least to watch the fire as it spreads but call the fire department as quickly as you can.

Is the fear or apprehension you are experiencing related to a genuine problem or is it a habitual pattern of worry about something that is not that big a matter one way or the other?

If a reaction of fear and worry is some old bad habit of counter-productive wheel spinning, it may be hard to change that habit. But it is important that the process of changing these old reflexes be engaged.

The real challenges of life are difficult enough.

All the available energy you have needs to be used as clearly and skillfully as possible for the difficult efforts of meeting whatever may be the core challenges and fears of your present life.

There will be occasions when a great deal of time and awareness need to be applied with care and skill when considering various future options and scenarios. The focus on the moment is not to say that you do not think about the future, but rather that you are aware when you are thinking of the future and doing so with as much calm and skill as possible as a way to reduce wasted energy.

What is important is that you know the difference between worrying about something that really may never happen and a genuine problem that you need to spend quality time thinking about and for which a real plan of action is needed.

Also, it is important to learn how not to spend a lot of time worrying about something if it will take another few days or longer before you even know if there is a problem or not.

9.

In this work of discerning which fears are excessive or compulsive and which are reasonable and justified it will help to keep remembering you can further engage your efforts with awareness, concentration, and compassion in this way.

You can touch your experiences of both excessive and justifiable fears and any present feelings of inferiority or inadequacy with awareness, patience, compassion, and acceptance.

Being more aware and making the conscious decision to infuse an experience with compassion, patience, and kindness will begin to transform the experience. As you learn the discipline of coming back to the present, you can more readily determine what needs to be done now as compared with what can be dealt with tomorrow or at some other appropriate time. Rather than just continuing to spin your wheels like a car stuck in a rut, you can stop and take the time to come up with a new plan, or to ask others to help so you can get the car moving again.

As the clarity of mind continues to develop, it will be more possible to see which fears are excessive and which fears are reasonable and need your near-term attention.

None of this is to imply that outgrowing old habits of excessive hand-wringing and wheel-spinning is easy. What is being said is that it is important to know when you are engaged in such counter-productive efforts. It is important to begin to learn how to dissolve these cycles by the substitution of more skillful efforts. What needs to be done? What can be done? What resources are needed? Are there any trustworthy people you know of who are able and willing to help?

As with all practices, be patient with your efforts in these regards, yet work as diligently as you reasonably can to develop more effective and more skillful habits and reflexes.

Often, when you are able to return to the present and are able to be more compassionate in the present, you will find that the present moment is good, or good enough. You will realize that you will be able to deal with whatever problem needs tending to as the situation continues to unfold.

As you relax into the present, to the degree that this is possible, you can make an important discernment. You can discern if you really cannot relax very much. If that is the case, then let that be all right as well. You may need to simply let it be completely acceptable that you are feeling anxious and distressed if that is what you are feeling and if those feelings cannot be readily assuaged. *It may be very important to make sure you do not make things worse by feeling bad that you somehow can't "just relax" or "let go of it," whatever "it" may be.*

> What is important is that if you cannot relax or let go, then that is all right as well. Over time you will learn how to do so.

Talking to trusted friends or engaging in skillful forms of exercise or positive recreational play such as Frisbee or volleyball or long walks, if such options happen to be available, will also support the de-escalation of anxiety. If you realize that you are caught up in some measure of worry or anxiety over some minor or imaginary problem, then you can begin to learn how to interrupt the habitual worry before it escalates.

If you determine that a surge of fear and worry is a justified reaction to a serious problem or threat, then you can simply acknowledge that this problem or threat is real and does need to be dealt with. You can then begin to proceed to discern what needs to be done.

In either case you can begin to see how it is possible to begin to substitute confidence and sound practical problem-solving skills for unskillful, hand-wringing worry.

10.

A third practical problem-solving skill is to experiment with cultivating a general level of confidence that you can meet the genuine challenges of your practical and spiritual life.

Regardless of your actual track record in a given matter, it will be helpful to just experiment in a general way with feeling more confident that you really can triumph over the challenges of your life. It is true that you really may not know how you will actually overcome a tough challenge, but a developing sense of confidence and positive self-image will greatly improve your process and results.

You do not actually need to be more confident to start with this effort although it would be good if this shift in attitudes is possible.

It is enough to simply imagine what it would be like to feel calmly confident and to engage this effort in creative imagination until you more clearly realize that feelings of greater confidence are really possible for you.

You can begin this effort by simply imagining, "What would it feel like to be more confident on a regular basis?"

You can begin to add the practice of feeling more confident in your own abilities and self-worth as an addition to your developing practice of offering love and compassion towards your own life.

It is simple. More confidence will help diffuse excessive anxiety and enhance your abilities to respond to justifiable fear.

11.

In all of these matters there is another general consideration that is a primary driver of a great deal of the fear, worry, and deep-rooted sense of inadequacy that besets many of us. This general consideration is that many people have not actually made the transition from childhood and adolescence into adult maturity regardless of how old they may be.

The reasons for this may be quite understandable given the role models that many children see before them in their family and society or the trauma they have experienced in their life. Whether the causes are understandable or not, the end result is the same.

Many people have a strong need to try to hide from, dodge, or otherwise try to escape from the problems and the responsibilities of their adult life. This tendency always has the same outcome.

More trouble and more fear.

Many persist even into later stages of life hoping someone else will come along and solve their problems with a magic wand or lottery ticket or take care of them somehow.

Sadly, this tendency becomes self-fulfilling. If people are trying to dodge the realities of their adult life, they will tend not to have very good problem-solving or decision-making skills. The poor results that come from the application of poor practical problem-solving skills further undermines people's confidence in themselves. The poor results of a poor process seem to confirm the low opinion they already had about their ability to meet life head on and to survive, let alone to thrive.

All the meditation books in the world will not help you if you are generally unwilling to face and to embrace the simple fact that adult life often has a welter of responsibilities and pressures that are hard to deal with for which there often is no ideal solution available.

Accepting the hard work of adult life and the various responsibilities that go with the freedom and joys of adult living is not a small step.

As is the case with all truly elemental practices, it is important to be patient with yourself, yet to work as diligently as you reasonably can. To one degree or another, it seems the occasional desire or urge to regress to an infantile state where there are no responsibilities persists for most of us throughout life, at least from time to time. But a very good beginning with this general effort is to become aware of any tendencies to hide from problems or to escape into some dreamland or addictive behaviors or to engage in magical thinking. It is a good beginning to be aware of any unrealistic wishful thinking that somehow genuine problems will just go away without any real effort or sacrifice or discipline.

Monitoring these interior wishes, urges, or undercurrents is another good way to practice the cultivation of mindful awareness.

Over time individuals can realize in what ways they are trying to dodge the challenges and responsibilities of adult life and begin to realize that this dodging is very much a dead-end path.

One of the major tests to see if you are caught in this web is to see to what degree you are willing to take responsibility where responsibility needs to be claimed and to openly face the genuine challenges of your life, especially when the outcome may be quite uncertain.

Can you stop blaming others when others are not to blame?

Are you responsible for any poor or terrible choices that contributed to whatever the general suffering or specific issue at hand may be? Perhaps there is nothing that you have done wrong or maybe there is. But if there is, then it is important to know this and to take responsibility for what you have done or failed to do or say.

If you do have genuine responsibility for wrong done to others which created problems for you and others, then claim that responsibility and enter into the efforts of confession and atonement as needed.

Once again, it is not so important that you know right away what to do about that responsibility. It is enough that you begin the process by just naming and owning your role in the situation and forgiving yourself and then getting ready to figure out what reasonably can be done.

The process begins with a simple naming of the problem.

It is important to engage this process without self-reproach or harsh judgment of self for poor choices of the past as this reproach or harsh judgment of self will only delay progress.

The time will come soon enough when you will have to make decisions about what needs to be done or at least what can be done next to face up to the genuine challenges of your current life.

The time may come when you need to seek the forgiveness of others and to forgive yourself, but harsh feelings of self-reproach, guilt, or shame will only siphon off needed energy. But for now taking responsibility and simply turning and facing genuine problems whose outcome is uncertain is the first real step out of most quagmires.

The trick is, as noted earlier, to begin by naming the problem out loud without immediately trying to jump into the solution which really may not be clear for a while. Over time you will begin to see what the next right thing is that you actually need to do or can do to deal with real trouble. But in the beginning it is enough to claim that responsibility that is yours to claim.

It is enough neither to claim more responsibility for a situation than what is yours to claim, nor to hide from whatever may be the appropriate level of responsibility by denying whatever role you may have played in creating an unfavorable situation.

Beginning to experiment with the simple practice of believing in your ability to face the genuine challenges of your life will also be of vital importance. Expressing and feeling a genuine sense of confidence and faith in one's general abilities to meet the challenges of their life can be as simple as this:

"I can face the challenges of my life and do what I can one small step at a time."

"I may not succeed in quite the way I may hope, or I may succeed in ways I cannot foresee at present but I can make the very best efforts I am capable of."

"I no longer need to be prevented by old fears from taking reasonable steps forward."

12.

It is in the trenches of harsh struggles when many come up against the key question of whether they do or do not believe in God and the divine assistance.

Those who do believe in God, or who are willing to explore the possibility that God is somehow present and available for strength and guidance, can practice the following simple efforts.

They can continue to remember, and remember again, that they now know how to touch the experience of their fear with compassion, awareness, patience, and clarity.

They can begin to diffuse and disperse their experience of fear by turning to a sincere reflection on what strength, guidance, and inspiration God may offer to help them get through hard trials.

They can consent to be available to experience more clearly the living presence of God's love and care in their life. They can see how this living presence can help them do what needs to be done. For those who believe in God, *or are at least willing to explore such beliefs*, they can take the time to consider how faith in God and immortal love and life can help diminish fear at the very depths of their life.

What is not being suggested is some sugary or gooey faith that everything will work out all right, although most things usually do work out sooner or later. What is being suggested is a faith that, by opening more innocently to God's help, sustenance, and living presence, *you can get through whatever happens, regardless of the outcome.*

Those who do not believe in God will approach the amelioration of fear and anxiety in different ways. For them the reflections are centered upon how to have deeper faith in those values and beliefs they do accept and how these teachings can help them to diminish fear and enhance well-being. They can continue to observe how all experiences are impermanent and that therefore fear and anxiety and the conditions that give rise to fear and anxiety will not last forever. In short, they can wait till the storm passes without getting caught up in a stressful and anxious state. They can continue to work carefully with the friends and teachers who are important to them to obtain suggestions about how to deal with fears and anxieties.

They can more deeply embrace their belief that they need to face their problems more or less alone and seek to summon the will and cultivate the skill to do so. While this perspective will not work for everyone, for those who engage this perspective with skill, it is a powerful practice.

Whether you believe in God or not, whichever of these two basic views of life you are most drawn to is the one to explore more fully.

13.

A fourth practical skill is to learn to reach out to others to see if they are able and willing to offer any real support or aid or guidance that will help you.

Who knows how many people there are who have rejected the very help they needed, but the number is a very high one and it grows every day.

It is true that seeking help is often not quite as easy as one would hope.

There are many people who either do not care or who would not help if asked. There are others whose attempts to help would only make matters worse. But there is also a great deal of compassion, skill, and people who really are willing to help if they can. *If you are willing to take some early risks with faith, then take the risk of believing and having faith that there are some people who can and will help. Keep your eyes open for those who can offer meaningful assistance.*

The more sincerely you search for help without pre-conditions, the more likely it is you will find the help you need. Why this is true may not be clear, *but the sincerity and humility of your search has a direct bearing on the quality of the outcome of your search.*

What is important to remember is that the more serious a problem is the more likely it is that the problem has been developing for a long time and will be dealt with only by a long-term effort. The more serious the problem is the more likely it is that the only way through it is to be humble and open enough to ask for help and to accept that competent help which is offered.

If you reach out to people who let you down or who do not come through for you or outright betray you, don't be too discouraged, although that is easier to say than to do. Just keep looking for good-quality help and assistance, and make sure you are truly open to recognizing good help when it does come and to accept and fully cooperate with that genuine help.

14.

A fifth practical skill is to improve the ability to write out the pros and cons of any important decision rather than just letting the whole set of problems spin around and around in your head in some vague, racing fashion.

Writing down the reasons to do something and the reasons for making a different decision can be extremely helpful. You will begin to organize your thoughts, and this will lower stress and tension, which will help make it more likely that your intuitive skills can kick in.

You will begin to realize there are some points that you need more information about before you can really make a decision, and you can then endeavor to seek out that needed information. Learning how to stall for time as you gather information needed to fill in the decision-making process may, at times, be a mildly disingenuous tactic, but nevertheless it is a very helpful skill to know how to use well. This stalling is not to be confused with avoidance of making decisions. Rather, legitimate stalling tactics are employed to complete the information-gathering process that is necessary for the full evaluation of important alternatives.

Once the information necessary to review the important options is obtained, then the decision can usually be made fairly readily and with a heart that is more free and clear.

15.

A sixth practical skill is to break down large problems that may be overwhelming into smaller steps that are far more manageable. The more serious a problem or struggle is, the more likely it will appear to be overwhelming, which in some cases may be the simple truth of the situation.

What really is helpful, in addition to staying in frequent contact with those you are studying with, is to break the problem into small manageable steps and then to take those next steps that reasonably can be taken.

Often people have a great deal of fear and worry about what to do with some situation, and so they feel overwhelmed or they become stuck in a kind of gridlock of inaction and worry.

Once a practical small step is identified, then a person can move into taking that small step *which may be all they really have the strength to do as they try to move forward.*

It might be something very simple like doing the laundry or getting estimates for work you need done at the house or office. What is important is to take a small step in the right direction and to continue to identify the next small step to take.

Should you find yourself paralyzed by inaction or depression or procrastination, then it is all the more important to summon whatever willingness you have to reach out to whomever you trust the most for a bit of encouragement and support. Establishing meaningful contact with someone who believes in you and who does not judge you for the problems you have is an extremely effective way to break out of procrastination or depression.

Successfully completing some small steps also generates confidence and momentum for the bigger tasks that need to be undertaken. The confidence that arises from successfully completing small steps will further diminish fear, worry, and insecurity. This also will make it more possible, in general, to succeed with the more difficult aspects of the challenges you face.

If you can break big problems into small, doable steps, you will be surprised at how much can be accomplished.

16.

A seventh practical problem-solving skill is to further cultivate the physical health of the body and the mind by making additional efforts with the forms of exercise touched upon in the chapter "Sacred Exercise."

The specific benefits of any of these forms of activity will help wash away the sludge and tightness that develop in the muscles and joints and other tissues of the body as a result of stress. Clearing out this sludge and opening tight and constricted muscles, tissues, and joints will refine the quality of energy circulating throughout the nervous system and other systems of the body.

This is a major benefit.

Endeavoring to reform your diet to consume less caffeine, sugar, white flour, and other "comfort foods" will also help to increase health and lower stress.

In the modern world many earn their living from intellectual or office-based skills. During the day or at the end of the day or the week the mind is simply in overdrive with many concerns. Taking the time to restore deep rhythmic breathing through skillful exercise and sending oxygen and nutrient-rich blood through the body will be of real assistance to clearing the mind and calming the body. This will allow for a refreshment of self and perspective that will allow you to return more skillfully when it is time to take up again whatever work or challenge you have before you.

The same beneficial results will accrue from further efforts to speak openly and at a deeper level with whomever you have chosen as a counselor, mentor, or spiritual guide about that which is most pressing in your mind and life condition. Simply talking with a trustworthy and mature confidante who will listen to you without harsh judgment will lower the level of force and velocity of a wide range of conflicts and conflicting emotions and physical drives. If you need to consider other modes of treatment for high degrees of anxiety then do so.

17.

As you live and as you explore what faith may mean to you, it is important to understand that when you are afraid, don't pretend that you aren't, as though you were "beyond all that" just because you have made some good commitments to meditation.

Be aware of the fear in your life whether it is excessive, neurotic, or compulsive or whether it is some very justified fear related to a very real difficulty.

If you really are not able readily to relax or calm down, it will only make matters worse if you feel bad that you are unable to "let it go." It will only make things worse if someone implies you should "just relax" when in fact that is exactly what you are unable to do at present.

What will help is to be aware when fear and worry have begun to escalate and to remember you can reach out to the counselor or mentor you are working with or friends you are close to.

Find people who understand what it is like for a person who is not able to calm down or relax very readily even if they want to. Find people who will not judge you for being afraid and who know that affirming you and your experience will help you lower stress over time.

Seek the best help you can and learn to listen in silence for the difference between how it feels when you hear a teaching that seems to be true as compared with how it feels when you hear a teaching that seems to be false.

18.

It is simple.

The mind and the body can truly let go and settle into the deepest experiences of peace only when fear has been diffused at depth. For this reason it is essential to find healthy ways to diminish fear at the depths of one's being. Better practical problem-solving skills combined with the other practices already offered will help to make a very real beginning and you can discern how to proceed from there.

None of this is meant to imply that this work is easy or quick.

The world is often a dangerous and violent place, and many people are right to be concerned that their physical and emotional safety and that of those they love are by no means assured.

Many others struggle with loneliness and significant problems with love and sexual fulfillment, or depression or addiction. The fear that they will never find a way out of these traps can be very formidable indeed.

Many find out too late they have made a bad marriage and realize they cannot stay in the marriage. They may be living with high levels of fear that they cannot afford to really leave the marriage even if that is the only viable choice in a bad situation.

Many are struggling to live with the fears that arise from difficult medical problems or not having any medical insurance coverage or not being able to find decent medical or psychological services even if they do have coverage.

Many are faced with the fear of badly destabilized financial conditions in their company or are afraid they may soon lose their job when there are not a lot of jobs to be had. Those who live in war zones, refugee camps, homeless shelters, or violent neighborhoods live with the constant and very reasonable fear of crime and violent attack.

Those who have been beaten or abused in childhood or who have been the victim of rape or other violent attack have been traumatized. They live with the destabilizing knowledge of how violent this world can be and in the very real knowledge that the same thing could happen again if they were to let their guard down or simply be in the wrong place at the wrong time.

Unscrupulous politicians and ruling cliques of all stripes have learned they can rise to power if they can successfully manipulate the fear and anger of the masses by demonizing enemies within the state and outside the state. Hundreds of millions are regularly caught up or swept away in the wake of these tides and whirlpools of fear and manipulation.

Added to this general list is the fear many experience about the possibility of a long painful decline of the body or real problems with poverty in their final years.

Added to all these general problems is the fact that many people grow up in religious cultures that distort the nature of God by hurling constant threats of eternal torture and damnation at the masses as a way to whip up their fears. For many the fear of eternal damnation or endless cycles of rebirth and death at the base of the psyche is not a small set of fears to try to live with. What could be worse than unholy religious teachers seeking to gain or hold on to positions of wealth, privilege, and prestige by scaring children and adults with threats of eternal punishment? Are we to believe that God is some vicious warden of a gruesome prison from which there is no reprieve? What kind of image of divine love do those who offer such teachings have in their heart and mind?

With all these impacts, no wonder many people are riddled with fear and anxiety. No wonder that more than a few become twisted into murderous impotent rage.

With all the violence and suffering that scars the life of so many in the world, who can blame anyone for doubting that a loving God is the foundation of all existence? Given the hypocrisy and error of so many religious leaders and believers, who could blame anyone for simply walking away from religion and faith with disgust, scorn, or indifference?

Yet if there were nothing more than the unpredictable violence and suffering of nature and human life, then why would anyone even consider that God is the foundation of all existence?

But there is more to life and nature than violence and suffering. There is also very real beauty and wonder in nature and the love, kindness, charity, and heroic service by individuals and organizations.

If there were only hypocrisy, error, and mediocrity in religion and religious cultures, then thinking people might do well to simply allow these diseased cultures to vanish over time. But there are other important aspects of religion and religious people's lives that witness to irreplaceable truths. For one example, religions are the inspiration for many of the very highest levels of artistic creativity. For another there is the solemn majesty of sacraments, cathedrals, simple chapels, and the mysterious quality of those spiritual people who have been true to the best traditions of their religious culture.

For all these reasons the issues of faith and belief are neither easily joined nor quickly dismissed by anyone who has made a commitment to seek truth, wherever the search for truth may lead.

Yet a difficult challenge remains for many. Is there a way to benefit from the truth and faith of a more spiritual life so as to experience a richer sense of beauty and connection without being damaged by the hypocrisy and dysfunction of particular religious cultures?

Is it better to choose to live in faith that God is present even if one may often not be at all able to explain how this could possibly be true?

Or is it better to endeavor to proceed towards liberation with faith in those teachings which say there is no such thing as God or a permanent self or soul?

Is there some other form of belief other than these two primary choices which is the best choice for you?

Please know that whatever choices you feel are right for you, the best wishes are offered for the completion of your journey.

19.

Whatever answers you come to with regard to such reflections on faith, fear, and doubt these few questions are useful:

> How can finding a vision of life you can have faith in help you to further diminish both fear and doubt?

> How can finding a vision of life you can have faith in, and deeper commitments to that faith, also help you diminish excessive desire?

> How can finding a vision of life you can have faith in, and then making deeper commitments to that faith, help you also to diminish the inflamed aspects of self and ego?

> How can the efforts to diminish fear, excessive desire, and the inflamed aspects of self and ego support the efforts to pierce the thick veils of illusion that prevent a person from perceiving the true nature of self and being?

These are good questions. These are true questions. These are simple questions.

Faith and Fear

Part 1

Basic Definitions and Choices

1.

As noted, one of the many benefits of the preceding practices is they do not require a person to believe in God or any one religion unless they freely wish to do so. Nor is there any explicit or implicit assertion that a person should not believe in God as though such beliefs were misguided fantasies.

This is important because many people are not sure what to believe.

All they are sure of is they do not want someone to demand they accept teachings on faith if they do not understand or agree with those teachings. While there is a genuine benefit to willingly accept certain teachings on faith, for such acceptance and faith can lead to understanding, many simply are not willing to do this. They really need some kind of evidence they can touch and hold before they feel they can make a commitment to believe. Given the very real problems, confusing vagueness, conflicted messages, and raw, violent dysfunction in many faith traditions this is a reasonable need.

In the simple path the evidence offered that can be touched and held is the evidence found in the personal experiences that arise from a sincere and diligent application of the most basic practices. In these personal experiences, you can weigh and measure according to your own criteria whether these experiences speak to, or at least hint at, truths you are willing to explore.

It is hoped the preceding practices and the ones which now follow are efforts most people can readily agree are reasonable and positive efforts to try. The benefit of doing so is that these simple practices, if cultivated with reasonable diligence, will be enough to generate at least early stage experiences of peace and clarity.

It is these early stage experiences of peace and clarity that become the living evidence and confirmation that one has chosen a good general direction to move in.

The living example of others who are further along the path than you are, along with venerable commentaries from ages past, will continue to reinforce that perception. The value of the best commentaries from ages past is an ongoing support to discernment, even if some of the passages and images are distinctly unhealthy or mistaken and need to be set aside.

From the felt evidence and confirmation of the early stage experiences of peace and clarity you can make the following decision: *"Does it make sense to trust and have faith that more decisive and consistent commitments to these general values and practices will yield ever more tangible experiences of peace and clarity?"*

This is a good early step of faith to consider working with.

As noted, these early thresholds of peace and clarity can be attained without asking a person to believe in any doctrine they either do not understand or cannot freely accept.

Nor is there any point in the future when people will be asked, or required to believe in any doctrine they do not freely come to believe makes natural sense to them.

This is the simple path.

2.

For those who are not sure what to believe, being willing to observe each moment more clearly and more innocently is a good place to begin this way of searching.

Sitting in stillness, silence, and emptiness on a regular basis will help cultivate better skills with mindful awareness. Regular practice will help people's awareness to deepen, over time, into concentrated awareness. All of this work will give rise to more penetrating insights.

The consistent engagement of subtle forms of exercise such as Yoga or T'ai Chi will help heal and tone the body as will the general efforts to adopt a healthier diet.

Cultivating compassion as a way to diminish anger and harsh judgment will help diminish any glaring experiences of stress and agitation that may be active in one's mind. The mind will further calm and clear.

Admitting freely and clearly when you have done something wrong to others and making amends will diffuse pangs of guilt and shame. The mind will further calm and clear.

Cultivating practical skills in the careful step-by-step process outlined in the preceding chapter will help a person begin to face more openly and diminish more skillfully their fears and anxieties. These practical skills will also help a person take the active steps needed to address whatever hardships and struggles may be present in their day-to-day life. All of this will further aid in the general effort of diminishing fear.

However messy and tentative one's practice and discipline may be at first, more tangible experiences of peace and clarity will continue to develop.

To the thresholds of peace and clarity that arise from these beginning practices the following reflections on ways to diminish doubt by searching for a vision of life and faith you can freely accept are now added.

3.

Faith is a form of confidence.

Faith is a growing sense of confidence that stronger commitments to the practices and values that have helped you so far will lead to increasingly deeper experiences of peace, insight, and clarity.

Reflections on the virtue of courage, and a willingness to be more courageous, will also bolster a sense of strength and confidence which in turn will further diminish fear and doubt.

Any lingering doubts about whether there is any such thing as truth, meaning, and purpose in this life will steadily lose their force and charge.

Nagging doubts that one is trapped in a prison of suffering that has no real end will also recede, for you will see and feel that suffering has begun to abate. Even if life continues to present difficult challenges or troubling emotional states, the seeds of real hope that genuine triumphs are possible will generate fresh energy and stamina. As one gains a general confidence they will be able to attain very worthwhile goals; they will begin to make stronger efforts which in turn will generate more momentum towards those goals.

Even if you continue to make very poor decisions from time to time, or if your life is beset by very real hardships, a growing sense of hope, confidence, and progress will develop.

This hope will further weaken the force and charge of various fears and anxieties.

For faith is a form of hope.

The hope is that real freedom is possible and closer than it was before.

4.

None of this is to imply that this process is some automatic or linear progression.

For those who have known real torment and hardship in their life, and whose best efforts to date have not yielded the kinds of benefits they had hoped for, the way forward may often be clouded with despair and high levels of anger and frustration. For those who have struggled to resist suicidal urges or violent impulses towards others over many years of their life, it may seem like one will be beset by such thoughts indefinitely.

It is just that this simple process will give people a context in which to conduct their search, however steep their path may be, without asking them to believe in teachings they really do not understand or accept. This by itself will relieve quite a bit of stress and tension for those with passionate and ardent natures who cannot find any way to understand or accept certain teachings they encounter.

The simple path is like a stairway that has only one stair.

As you step on the first stair the second appears, sturdy and true.

As you step on the second stair the third appears.

After a dozen stairs you will see much more of the rest of the stairway. You will also gain a glimpse as to how high the stairway extends although it extends so high you will not be able to see the top quite yet.

5.

When one is ready, and each person is the only one who can decide when they are ready, they can explore basic decisions with regard to a vision of life they can freely have faith in.

A person may come to believe it makes sense for them to choose a life of faith in God, or at least to explore this possibility, and if so which vision of God's life and nature to have faith in.

Or, a person may feel called to believe it is wise to explore an atheist path of knowledge, wisdom, or science that is not centered in God or a belief in the immortality of the soul.

If a person chooses to freely explore what it would be like to really believe in God, they can begin the process of discerning what might be the true nature of God's life and divine consciousness. They can also begin to ask God for help and guidance in their search even if they don't really know how to ask or who it is they are asking.

Some may wish to explore a cerebral and somewhat abstract notion that God's nature is very general and without attributes of any kind. This view is a good general description of the nature of Brahman or the Absolute in many portions of the Hindu tradition or the Christian Apophatic method of meditation as described by Dionysus the Aeropagite.

Others may be inclined to follow a God-centered path that teaches that divine love is the defining attribute of God's nature. This view is a good general description of the faith held by Jews, Christians, Moslems, and many other faith traditions.

Still others may decide it makes sense to explore the search for liberation without any belief in God or the soul. For those so inclined, a serious study of such traditions as Theravada Buddhism, Zen, or secular humanism would be some good choices to consider.

What is important is that a steady engagement of the earlier practices and those which follow will generate, sooner or later, increasingly more palpable experiences of peace and consolation.

These deeper consolations and experiences of sacred peace and beauty will give rise to additional confidence and faith that one has found a true path that leads to a true and very valuable destination. Doubt and skeptical apprehension will be more completely transformed into confidence and hope.

The confidence that arises from these consolations will also help people face more of their fears and opportunities. It will be easier to believe they can better cope with the pressing hardships of their life as well as the opportunities life also presents.

Increasingly deeper experiences of concentration, insight, love, and peace will arise.

This greater confidence along with the inspirations of simple hope and refreshment that arise from steadily increasing experiences of peace and insight will further diffuse fear.

It is in this way that practices which generate experiences of peace and clarity will help diminish any doubts that real freedom is possible in this life.

It is in this way that practices which generate experiences of love and human decency will diminish lingering uncertainties about which general path leads to light and truth.

6.

The following efforts to engage pure imagination will also help.

Take the time to imagine what it would feel like to really live without fear.

None of this is to imply that one should undertake some rash or impulsive or foolishly dangerous thrill-seeking actions.

What is being said is that as you imagine what it would feel like to live without fear, it will become clear how beneficial it would be to diminish fear at the deepest levels of the psyche. Admittedly, attaining such states of fearlessness usually will require real work and patience. Furthermore, actually living like this all the time may not be too realistic, but one can cultivate the conditions where this diffusion of fear at depth can actually happen at least for periods of time, and one can proceed from there.

The general point is that when fear is diffused at depth, the mind can relax and let go at deeper levels.

This deeper relaxation and more complete letting go will allow noticeably more pure experiences of peace, clarity, and calm to develop.

With the skills that arise from such training and experiences you will gain the insights needed to pierce the veils of illusion. It will be possible to perceive and experience more tangibly a clearer sense of the true nature of self and being even if it remains difficult to describe exactly what is this sense of true being they have perceived.

A person will come to know that what they have heard is actually true: the profound depths of peace in contemplative states are real and exceptionally pure and refreshing.

Whatever questions of life or truth which remain unanswered at this point, and there will be many, will be less and less relevant.

7.

While this way of cultivating faith is much more open than many, it remains important to be clear that not all paths lead to the summit of the mountain. This is true even if quite a few of those paths have a big sign that says they do lead to the summit.

What is essential is that only those paths which emphasize the importance of offering love towards one's own life and to all beings as a central tenet are worthy of serious consideration. However difficult it may be at times to be willing to forgive all offenses and to actually offer love and compassion to all beings, this is the essential feature that any true path will have.

Still, as noted earlier, this is a goal one can work towards gradually and at a realistic pace.

The choice that every person needs to make and the choice that only each person can make for their life is this:

> *Are you willing to improve your present abilities to give and to receive, and to feel the giving and receiving of love?*

Are you willing to see if there is a way to offer love to all beings past, present, and future as a central commitment of your life and practice of silent meditation? Whatever other differences may exist between venerable religions or philosophies will become less and less relevant as one's commitment and skill with this essential practice develops.

It is simple.

Unconditional love will heal and transform the wounded self and heart.

Unconditional love will also transform the faculties of reason and open more widely the mysterious channels of intuition and empathy in ways that make the discernments of faith and the perception of true being more possible.

Unconditional love will refine the faculties of consciousness so one is able to perceive more clearly the true nature of self and being, or at least to see this river as though standing on a nearby cliff.

More tangible glimpses of the true nature of being, even if it remains difficult to describe such experiences, will form the basis of deeper faith in a vision of life a person can commit to. At some point a person can discern if it makes sense to explore the creative power of unconditional faith in the vision of life and being they are exploring. The greater range of personal experience and insight that will have arisen by this point will help in this discernment. What is important, what is difficult about the spiritual life is this: *Deep faith in the teachings you feel will lead to liberation will be needed quite a while before you actually have all the evidence you need to support such a choice.* In fact, it is a commitment of deeply held faith in the path and goal you have chosen that is needed to generate both the evidence you seek and the desired fulfillment. These comments are offered with the assumption that you have chosen a good path to a good goal, which is to say a path that is centered in unconditional love for all beings.

Helping people cultivate a certain richness of personal experience they can use as their base of evidence as they consider taking greater risks with faith before all the evidence is available, is a primary theme of the simple path. So too is the notion that commitments of faith can be incremental in nature as experience and evidence accrue to support ascending degrees of faith.

What you can count on is that a diligent commitment to unconditional love and related practices will give rise to the tangible personal experiences needed to aid your discernment.

8.

The following suggestions will help people lower the stress of doubt and confusion in their life which can be a significant constraint on their search for a sense of faith they can freely embrace.

If you really are not sure whether God does or does not exist, or what God's nature may be, it is important never to try to resolve such questions by brute force of intellect.

It is enough to honor the different and conflicting perspectives you have on such questions.

It is enough to let the choices you are considering, assuming they are at least generally plausible choices, to have space within you to live and to be part of you. Spend real time with each credible possible choice. See if you can further cultivate your understanding of that way of believing as a way to see what experiences may arise from following that path.

It is enough to touch both the experiences of your doubts, your confusion, and your experiences of faith with awareness, patience, acceptance, and compassion.

This acceptance and honoring will diminish the sense of tension and strain of not knowing what to believe and not knowing where to find relief or the path that leads to deep healing experience.

Just this lowering of tension over not knowing what to believe will be helpful.

From this acceptance and honoring you will be creating the space and calm within you for more profound insight and more authentic revelation to emerge. From this process, and from ongoing study, and from seeking counsel with mature guides, a clearer conception of what is a true path will emerge that will make sense to you.

At times you may feel it is wise to revisit some beliefs you previously rejected.

At others times you may feel it is wise to set aside some beliefs you had previously made strong commitments to.

None of this is to imply that this is some easy path where everything just works out, although sooner or later most hard challenges and questions are resolved.

A highly principled search for faith is not without difficulties, and the challenges and pains of life and nagging doubts do not magically drift away. Still, you will find there are greater reservoirs of experience and strength within you and around you than you were previously aware of.

You will find ever more creative ways to respond to the legitimate struggles of your life and heart.

You will also find ever more creative ways to respond to the various conflicts and needs of those you love the most and in the society in which you live.

This is a good hope. This is a true hope. This is a simple hope.

9.

As you reflect on what is a true path for you, the following set of filters will help as you make your discernment of faith.

Are your beliefs helping you to diminish excessive desire and restless aching hunger or not?

Are your beliefs leading you to higher-grade skills with love, respect, charity, tolerance, patience, courage, humility, and calm?

Are you at least a little less irritable and impatient or do you find yourself still frequently boiling over with irritability and rage?

Are your beliefs leading you to more or less peace and freedom?

Are your beliefs helping you to develop more advanced skills with non-violent conflict resolution?

If the answer to any of these questions is no, then it makes sense to ask these questions:

> Is the problem simply that you are not making the best efforts you can with the path you have chosen? Or is it possible you have not found or chosen the right set of beliefs?

What is important to remember in this discernment is this: *Different people may really need different beliefs and expressions of faith. Different people may really need different forms of practice and worship.*

It is not just that cultures are different. The brains, the structure of the unconscious, and the ways of processing information and experience vary significantly depending on people's genetic make-up and cultural grouping. To say it more simply; brain chemistry varies from one person to another. Consequently, very different ways of searching and different aspects of belief will be needed even though certain core values and virtues such as love, personal integrity, and faith will be common to any valid path.

In truth it may be that differences between people's brains and the functions of their conscious and unconscious faculties may be the underlying reason why there are very different religious cultures in the world. This is another fascinating theme for further research in contemplative studies.

10.

The following open-minded comparisons of the advantages and disadvantages of different beliefs are offered for those who are wondering how to decide whether God does or does not exist.

A belief that God does exist and that divine love is the most important aspect of God's nature has these major advantages. If one believes in this way they can seek to open their heart and mind to divine love and to the Lord of heaven and earth for guidance and sustenance in good times and bad. They can begin to trust more completely and settle into increasingly deeper states of assured faith that they will live forever embraced in immortal love and life. A true and sure faith that one will live forever embraced in divine love will take much of the sting out of the passing hardships of life. This is particularly true of the general challenges of contemplating one's final years and the death of the body. After all, if one genuinely believes they are destined to live forever embraced in perfect peace and love, then the transient pains of this life, even the severe ones, will be far more bearable. These are real advantages.

But, those who believe God exists, and who believe that divine love is the most elemental aspect of God's nature, also encounter several major excruciating contradictions. *For many the most difficult is to find some way to explain why there is so much horrible suffering, natural disasters, and injustice in this world if divine love is the foundation of all life.*

This is a formidable challenge. A serious discernment of this issue can be a brutally painful conundrum to try to resolve which many never find any real way through. The only way most people of faith are able to live with this horrible contradiction is that the sharp pains of life are simply not so numerous or long lasting. In short, the lives of most are stable enough that they never really need to confront this question long enough to admit they have no real answer or to see the answers they have shattered by overwhelming suffering.

Certainly, many have offered certain traditional answers to resolve this sharp contradiction. The problem is that many, many people find these answers are at best only partially true and then in only limited contexts.

The rape and murder of children, the merciless violence of dictators and gangsters, birth defects, serious mental illness are flashing red lights of doubt for many. The sudden death of tens of thousands by natural disaster, or painful deaths by wasting disease are other great glaring question marks hovering over the teachings that divine love is the foundation of all life.

What does it matter if humans have free will, if your child has been kidnapped, raped, and tortured to death and you know the killer has gotten away and will do the same to other children?

What does it matter if humans have free will when you think of the fact that over a million of the people who died in Nazi concentration camps were children under the age of ten?

Even the most committed of believers in divine love can find themselves shaking and trembling and screaming at God in the aftermath of terrible disaster or devastating loss.

"How could you allow these things to happen?"

This is an important question.

For many the question of how to reconcile a notion of an all-loving God, with the bitter and excruciating nightmares of this world may be the most violent and unanswerable doubt they have. For those who do believe, and those who are struggling to believe, there are alternative ways to approach this painful question. But this question and these alternative approaches to this question are better addressed in a separate commentary to be written at another time. These other thoughts, due to their length and highly speculative reflections, might appear to be slanted too much in the favor of those who do believe, or are at least trying to believe that God is real and that divine love and immortal life are the most important attributes of God. For this reason the decision was made not to include these reflections in this present volume. This present volume is intended to maintain a studied and dispassionate neutrality to avoid the presence or undercurrent of belief one way or the other on important basic questions. The rationale for this neutrality is that those who might ordinarily stay away from spiritual literature may feel more inclined to follow the discussion as long as they know there is no undertow in favor of any one set of conclusions.

For now it is enough to acknowledge and fully honor the pain and tormented doubts that can arise in anyone who believes in God who has also been devastated by great suffering. Having opened their heart in tender faith and vulnerability to God's mercy, care, and love only to awake one day to find their life or their nation has been ripped apart, who could blame anyone for turning within or screaming at altars, "Where is your love and protection when I needed it the most?"

> "Where were you when my child was raped and tortured to death?"

> "Where are you when an elderly person lies writhing in pain for days, weeks, or years, in the final chapters of their life?"

For now it is enough to honor the suffering of all who have been driven by life's extremities to ask these questions as they search for the strength to continue, let alone the will to continue, in faith that God exists and cares.

For now, if this question or any similarly deep question is of searing and passionate importance to you, this will also help:

It is enough to be as fully aware of any and all conflicts you have about how divine love could possibly be the foundation of all life. It is enough to know that such doubts are completely understandable reactions to harsh suffering when you have tried to believe in God's love and care for your life and this world.

It is enough to be as fully aware of any heartrending, mind-numbing conflicts you have with the teachings or the actions of the church you belong to or one you are considering converting to.

It is enough to touch your experiences of conflict, doubt, anguish, and confusion with the most tender awareness, patience, acceptance, and compassion you can.

If or when serious doubt arises, do not pretend that this is not happening as though you were somehow more established in faith than you may be. We are human. The raw pain and suffering of this life is enough at times to shatter anyone's faith no matter how much meditation they have done or how often they have received sacraments with a pure and willing heart.

Look closely at any experiences of doubt and the crumbling of faith.

It is enough to draw upon your developing skills with awareness to observe the arising of doubt and despair if such experiences arise. It is enough to see in such cases if there is a way to extend your faith another few inches or hours. It is enough to honor both your doubts and your wish to find a way to cultivate faith in the midst of truly hard times.

It is enough to cry out to God with every ounce of anger, passion, and fear within you. For in the days or nights of unholy terror that can happen in this world, this crying out in sheer desperation may be the best and also the most those who believe can do.

"God help me." "Where are you?"

It is enough to seek the help of other mature people to get through whatever crises have arisen. The wise will not try to answer your questions or assuage your howling grief with bromides or platitudes. They know such cheap comments are of no use if your wife and children have just been killed by a drunk driver who walked away without a scratch. The wise will do what they can to bandage your wounds, to lessen your pain, to share your experience and walk with you until the pain passes as sooner or later it will. Then you and they can continue the search for better explanations to such painful riddles and better ways to diminish or at least more steadfastly endure the suffering of this life.

It is enough to try to open your heart and mind to God and joy and the suffering of this world as widely and innocently as you are able to *without trying to understand how these phenomena are supposed to interlace with one another.*

If you need to, then simply set aside any answers you have ever heard about how to understand the searing juxtaposition of images of God supposedly looking down from heaven and not intervening when a bleeding and screaming child is in process of being beaten to death by the drunken boyfriend of a negligent mother.

Set aside any answers that seek to trivialize the horror of such situations and see how you can open your heart and mind to God and to all the suffering children, men, and women of this world.

See how your practice can generate insight, courage, and wisdom that will allow you to protect more of the children of the world and to be the living hand of safety and kindness to all who suffer. Look as clearly and deeply as you can into the depths of your own heart and mind and as openly and honestly as you are able into the raw suffering of human life as well as the suffering of less complicated life forms of this world.

Come back, whether you are crying or bleeding, whether you are shaken or composed, to make fresh efforts with those beliefs and practices you do understand with which you know you could be making a better effort.

Keep searching for ever more creative ways to awaken a more healing experience of God's living presence even in the midst of real trouble. Keep searching for ever more creative ways to draw upon God's life and power to diminish more of the suffering of this burning planet.

You may not ever know the answers to your most important questions or then again you may.

But it will help to just clear your mind of all the teachings and answers that do not make any sense at all no matter how hard you try to embrace them and no matter how often others try to explain what appear to be grossly insensitive answers to serious questions.

What is more important is what is happening now. What help do you need to diminish any raw suffering in your life now? Over time you can come back if you wish to continue to reflect on whether God exists and if so whether God's nature is one of neutral indifference or perfect and immortal love and life.

For those who do believe in God, or are at least willing to explore that God may exist and may respond to human appeals, you can try this during times of serious doubt and personal struggle.

"God, help me through this dark night."

"God, where are you, what am I missing?"

"God, can't you see we are on the verge of being destroyed by savage and vicious aggressors? Help us to know what to do, or at least how to face the lions in the coliseum with courage and dignity."

"God, I do not know what are the best ways to come closer to you, but lead the way and I will follow."

"Send me a sign or intuition that helps me to know if you are here and how I can perceive your presence and draw upon your strength."

The key is not to ask for guidance only in times of great trial or occasionally on Sunday morning. The key is to reach out with openness to God throughout the days and nights of your life. Ask until you feel you either get confirmation that God does exist or you hear no answer and see no sign and conclude, at least temporarily, that there is no one there in the vast reaches of space.

Many people spend years studying their trade or profession, developing their business or perfecting their art or craft. Yet when it comes to the search for God, it is a few moments here and there punctured by a life of scrambling, pointless indulgence, and self-centered desires.

If you believe in God but do not feel God's presence, or if you are willing to open your heart and mind to see if God will reveal the divine nature to you, do not let this search be a hobby.

Ask with every ounce of strength you have. Ask as often as you are able.

If on the other hand you accept one of the traditional answers to the oft asked question, "How could there be a God in heaven who cares about us, when one sees the brutal nightmares of this world?" then best wishes to you. You have your path to walk. May the bright joy and enduring strength of your communities be a beacon and refuge to you and to many.

If you believe in God, however you decide the most difficult questions of God and human suffering, the work remains to be the same.

Let your day be a day of a hundred prayers.

How can your faith in divine love lead to greater understanding and experience?

How can you find ever more effective ways to diminish the suffering of this world and in whatever other worlds or realms may exist in the far flung reaches of time and space?

Still the questions can fairly be asked, "Wouldn't it be simpler to come to the conclusion that either there is no God, or if God does exist that he, she, or it has little concern for the suffering that crushes and destroys so many?"

Given the raw suffering and violence that scars the lives of so many in this world, no one could be blamed for doubting that this world was created or watched over by a loving God.

This is a reasonable doubt. Honoring the reasonableness of this doubt is actually one of the best ways to find a way through it, should you be inclined to try.

11.

Those who do not believe in God or divine love have the big advantage that they do not need to explain why there is so much horrible pain and suffering in the world. They just know that horrible suffering is a reality of this life as is the most tender joy and beauty.

It is enough for them to know that suffering, poverty, terrible accidents, old age, illness, and death are very real. While such people acknowledge that pain remains to be a real challenge, they also are clear it is very possible to diminish that suffering we generate within ourselves that badly exacerbates the pain of difficult situations.

It is enough for them to practice as diligently as they can when conditions are favorable so they will have better skills to cope when real hardship develops in their life.

But people who believe in this way also have very real stumbling blocks of their own.

They have to deal with the underlying belief there is no real point or meaning to this life other than to diminish as much of their suffering as they can. They have to make as much progress in this life so that when they are dead they remain truly dead and are never born again.

Is not this in reality what the doctrines of karma and reincarnation teach?

Is this not a stunningly bleak vision of life?

It is a vision that liberation, though possible, signifies nothing in any larger scheme of things and that liberation is just another random possibility as are the accidents of their life and the suffering and joys of this life.

Those who believe there is no God also have another major stumbling block. They need to face all of life's trials and hardships with only their own will power and whatever help they may get from other mortals they know, or from the teachings of their tradition.

This too can be a formidable challenge.

Who does not find themselves alone and afraid from time to time when none of their spiritual practices are helping them? Who does not find themselves shaken by the raw suffering of this life or with the searing knowledge of the violent horror and injustice inflicted on many?

In the deafening roar of bombs exploding around the fox hole, or in the doctor's office when a diagnosis of a terminal illness has just been delivered, who does not find themselves wishing that maybe God does exist and can help them through a painful and horrible death?

The general problem with believing that human will power is enough to attain full liberation is that the limitations of the individual will and human reason are very real.

Furthermore, there are many challenges a person faces, especially those suffering from mental illness or compulsive self-destructive desires that many are not able to address by their own will power. *For such people the nature of their malady is that the centers of will and volition are exactly the faculties that have become impaired.*

If you are able to diminish life threatening addictions or compulsions without believing in God or a higher power, then do so and all the best wishes for your efforts. But, if you find yourself in a situation where you feel you are not strong enough to overcome certain excessive desires by yourself, you can also consider asking or begging God for help even if you have ignored God up till now. This idea of turning to God in times of real crises even if you have no idea of who God is or whether God exists, and have lived a terrible and scandalous life up till now, is still a possibility.

You can steal away by yourself when no one is looking and get down on your knees and state your fumbling prayers, "God, help me through these troubles."

You can do this at any time if you find your usual coping skills are of no avail and you have nowhere else to turn.

12.

Still the question persists, "Does anyone actually gain liberation by their own efforts without the help of others or God?"

It is a fair question.

Even those who teach that one's own insight and will are sufficient for liberation also emphasize the importance of the example of illustrious predecessors, the power of transmitted teachings, and the value of community and common observance.

Who can say that the teachings of illustrious forebears and the support of community and common observance are not the ways a culture that claims to be an atheist culture draws unknowingly upon the divine resources embedded in the firmament of their community of like- minded people? Even if the members of that community do not use the word "God" in any way, shape, or form, who is to say that the helping hand of their teachings, their traditions, and their living exemplars is not the unseen hand of divine life simply not recognized as such?

For example when Zen teachers of the Boundless Way talk about the helping opportunities presented by the universe, it is not difficult to understand they are really talking about God even if they are not inclined to acknowledge this is what they are saying.

Who can say with certainty that those who believe the individual will is enough to achieve liberation are *not missing the true source of the inspiration for the teachings and the community they draw regularly upon?*

13.

For many the question continues to be important.

Is faith in God and God's grace the only power in the universe capable of transforming the badly-impaired human will and consciousness into a suitable condition where union with the divine is possible? Or, is faith that your own will power and the help of other mortals and the teachings of venerable masters of meditation are enough for a person to attain full enlightenment?

This is one of the seminal questions of the spiritual life and one of the major fault lines that separates certain traditions from one another.

The good news is that you do not need to know the answer to this question to make real progress with silent meditation and the cultivation of skill and wisdom.

It is enough to honor and bless any confusion you have with this or any other question.

It is enough to be mindfully aware of any conflicting views and doubts you have.

It is enough to touch all doubts and views you have with tender awareness, patience, acceptance, and compassion.

It is enough to honor and bless any truth and faiths you have come to believe are deeply true even if you may not be able to prove your beliefs in a scientific way.

Many will find a hybrid between the views that are centered on God's grace and those which emphasize that human will is enough. They will assert there are choices that a person must be willing to make to cooperate with God's grace, but that the agency of grace is the ultimate power needed for transformation.

Whichever of these paths you feel at the depths of your heart and mind are true is the path it makes sense to explore with greater faith and commitment and see what you find.

If the experiences and evidences you find confirm you are on the right path, then persevere as you have. If the experiences and evidences you find confirm that you are badly stuck, then it may make sense to explore shifting your beliefs to see if other beliefs will be more efficacious.

People following either path will have the same general challenges.

Life is often very difficult.

Suffering is real and often hard to diminish even with the best of efforts by the smartest and most dedicated people. Religious cultures and teachings may both greatly help and badly hinder the process of seeking relief. This is because mixed in with the irreplaceable truths and beauty of all well-developed ancient and modern spiritual cultures are serious errors and the worst kinds of hypocrisy to one degree or another. Sorting out the wheat from the chaff in the tradition you have embraced or are exploring may be very difficult and bewildering. Preserving that which is worthy of the old ways, while discerning how to set aside what needs to be left behind or renounced may also be quite difficult.

While many of the ancient and modern beliefs are enough to support the search for liberation, all of the ancient and modern systems of belief and knowledge are in need of significant reform.

Still, it is often far from clear what those reforms need to be.

What you can have faith in is this:

As you love, so shall you find.

You can have faith in love.

Faith and Fear

Part II

Simple Steps

14.

For those who continue to be uncertain how to proceed or which teachings are worthy and true there is good news.

If you do not feel comfortable taking the leap of faith that God does exist, or the leap into believing there is no such thing as God, there are some very nice small steps of faith that will help you find a path that is true for you.

The first is this:

> *At the center of your life there is a part of you that is good, true, and very creative. At the center of your life this matrix of who you are has been unfolding within you since birth.*

Whatever negative, self-centered, mean-spirited, or downright ruthless tendencies may exist in your life, you can have faith that the core of who you are is good and pure.

There may have been many times when you did not take time to notice the best that is within you, but there is time to change this. You can begin to listen more carefully for that still, small voice which is good and true within you. For the flame of that which is good and dignified within you cannot be extinguished in this life.

Anyone, no matter how evil they have been and how justly they deserve to be forcibly restrained or imprisoned, if necessary, by society, can choose at any time to change their life. Anyone can open their heart and make contact with that which is good and righteous within them.

Take the time to reflect back on your life. Search out the memories of the significant moments of your life when you had some experience that shaped your beliefs about the truth of your life in particular and of all life in general.

Look back at these different moments.

It may have been certain comments you heard from those relatives or friends you trust and love the most that struck you in a certain way that opened a certain door or possible path within you.

Or it may have been a beautiful melody of a hymn in some church service, or the inspiring highpoint of a sermon, or dharma talk. For some, such important epiphanies may have arisen when attending an art exhibit, or music festival, or learning for the first time of an elegant universal law or equation of physics.

Or it may have been some image that came to mind, from where you did not know, but which you knew was somehow a primal and important image for your life.

Or you may have read a passage in a book, or been moved by a certain scene in a movie, or some commentary on religion or some historical figure that seemed to allude to an elemental truth of life that was important for you to explore more carefully.

Or it may have been a particularly vivid and sacred image in a dream.

Look carefully over the long contours of your life.

You will see there have been certain moments of experience and awareness when you heard or saw something you felt was somehow deeply true whether you were able to respond to it at the time or not.

Look carefully and you will see that there have been many such moments beginning in early childhood extending through adolescence and into adulthood.

The more you look the more of these moments you will find. You will find a long string of these moments when a certain general vision of life or sense of truth, faith, charity, and beliefs began to emerge that caused you to develop your current views.

This continuum of important moments is a river within you that is still flowing.

By skillfully searching the past and finding those moments that formed who you are and what you believe and what sort of work you may do, will allow you to connect with the central core of character that has been unfolding within you since your birth.

This is a very good way to discern the long-term contours of what you believe is true whether that general direction is a God-centered way, or a path to liberation which has no belief in God.

By seeking to be in closer harmony with this unfolding nexus of your life, it will be possible to discern the way forward. For some it may mean a return to beliefs they once felt were true but which they abandoned. For others, they will feel a need to seek for the first time to be true to that which they had not taken full notice of before.

This sequence of moments, this continuum of experience and hope, will continue to unfold within you through the remaining stages of your life and, as many believe, after death.

By honoring that which is most true within you, you will come to greater levels of understanding and experience about the bigger questions of faith and life that at present remain quite unanswered. As experiences of peace, sacred beauty, and insight unfold within you, offer your consent that these experiences may become ever deeper and more clearly felt.

For faith is a form of consent.

15.

There is a second possible small step of faith for those not willing to take big leaps.

Take the time to uncover and dismantle any barriers to giving and receiving love that may have developed in your life.

Most people are unaware of the levels of anger, fear, mistrust, and need-for-control that are active in their life. These emotions prevent the more subtle experiences and intuitions from emerging and so a person's inner life is too constricted for any real progress to be made.

The general problem for many is that the pain of the first few years or decades of life was so acute they learned to live with high degrees of anger, fear, mistrust, guilt, and resentment as the general conditions of their life. In fact, they are often unaware that there is anything unusual about such high levels of anger, as so many around them feel much the same way. The troubles in many people's family life, or the society in which they were raised, were serious. For many there never was enough love, or at least not enough consistent love, for a stable sense of positive self-worth and security to develop.

Without any real experience of being able to trust in love and to feel this love, it is much more difficult for such people to have any sustaining experience of love. This in turn limits their ability to trust in general. The problem is at least some willingness to trust is needed for any real experience, love, and faith to develop, whether that faith is God-centered or not.

This shut-down state is especially common for those who were victimized, or worse, traumatized by others or saw those they love abused by another family member.

The levels of anger, fear, mistrust, and guilt that may be present within those who were deprived or traumatized can be so intense that many of life's more delicate feelings are just lost or short-circuited by the conflicting charges of these turbulent emotions.

As a consequence of such powerful emotions and tangled webs of anger and low self-worth, all relationships in childhood, adolescence, and adulthood tend to be more difficult and prone to serious conflicts. Tragically, the dominoes of unfulfillment keep falling. As there is little in the way of consistent love or real friendship or success in work relations, a bitter and cynical view of life seems to be confirmed in the lives of many.

Without healthy experiences of love and friendship, there is little of the joy and ease that are a part of healthy relations. As a result, many remain in a cramped, defensive, or arrogant posture.

The defensive armor and aggressive weaponry that many developed to protect the serious wounds in the vulnerable center of their life substantially impede any of the more sensitive feelings of life and sustaining care that otherwise could surface and be felt. This defensive armor and weaponry also further undermine one's abilities to cultivate healthy relationships. Experiences of sustaining mortal love and friendship remain elusive, or those relations that do come together are highly unstable or riddled with pain and dissatisfaction.

Whether one is drawn to a God-centered path or a Godless path of liberation, the effect is much the same. They may struggle for years with pain and depression and not really get anywhere with their practice of silent meditation, even with real effort and genuine sacrifice. Or, at least there is little in the way of discernible progress even if real changes are happening slowly within.

This can be a difficult set of life conditions to work out of. Anyone who finds themselves stuck in such a place will need to be careful to be as sincere as possible in their efforts to work free from such gridlock. But there is a consolation to this predicament. Those who begin their journey from such a difficult starting place are often the ones who reach the highest states once they get past the first few difficult stages.

The practices of affirmation of self and those you love the most will help dismantle these interior fortress walls and armaments so that it is easier to be in relationship with others. Thoughtful and sustained deliberations with counselors or mentors may also be needed to dismantle the armor that once was needed but now is a major impediment.

With the practice of affirmation and the insights of mature friends and mentors it will also be easier to let go of the need for rigid and inappropriate efforts to control other people. This will allow others to be more willing to be in relationship with the person who is laboring to do this work. This will also allow those people an individual cares for to accept more readily the friendship or love the troubled individual is attempting to offer.

Everybody wins.

The practices of affirmation and the openness to find ways to give and receive love, respect, and friendship more openly and skillfully will give rise to healthier relational experiences. One can explore these experiences of connection to see where they lead.

Some may come to believe that mortal love and friendship are templates for the relationship with God and immortal love and life.

Some will not feel this is true, but will realize more clearly how vital a support a community of friends, mentors, and co-workers can be in their search for truth, richness of experience, and liberation.

Each person will decide for themselves which of these basic views of life they feel is most true.

What you can count on is this:

> *As the blocks to giving love and the barriers to receiving love are dismantled, you will grow in mature insight, richness of life experience, and wisdom.*

Love is highly creative.

Love heals the wounded self at depth.

This healing will diminish doubt. It will be natural to consider that deeper faith in the transforming power of love and positive virtue will help you in your search. Regardless of the specific religious or philosophical tradition in which you live and express your deepening faith in love, you will know you have found a good path. You will also begin to trust more unreservedly that you have found a source for the strength needed to walk that path.

Both fear and doubt will be diffused at more elemental levels.

16.

There is another important aspect to this process of healing the self many will also need to give consideration to as part of dismantling the underlying tension in both the body and emotions.

This work is to become aware of any general feelings of fear and inadequacy that may be active in regard to a person's self-image and attractiveness or confidence as a sexual partner.

While those who feel called to the celibate way of life will process this work very differently than those who are living a sexually active life, the work remains to be an important means to heal the self at depth.

The sexual drives are so embedded in the central nervous system of the mind and body that you can be sure any feelings associated with the sexual drives go to the very root of the self. Fears of being unattractive or concerns about not being able to satisfy one's sexual partner so they will stay can create substantial tensions in the body and the emotions. Reviewing mindfully and talking openly with a trusted and skillful mentor about feelings you have related to sexual appetites and performance is another very helpful way to cultivate awareness. Few reflections will tell you as much about who you are at depth as this one.

Any messages heard in church or read in sacred texts that refer to the body and the sexual drives as being unclean or as part of one's inherently sinful nature add to the tensions of body and mind for many. *After all, if a person has very strong sensual desires, but is told again and again from pulpits or in commentaries on meditation that the desires of the body are fundamentally unclean, this conflict will have a very real impact on the psyche.*

Inappropriate comments or abusive behavior from family members make matters worse for those unfortunate enough to be damaged by such family dynamics.

Once again, though celibate people will process a review of the feelings they find associated with their sexual feelings and memories differently than will be the case for those who are sexually active, such a review is nevertheless needed. It is important to become conscious of any wounds to sexual identity and any harmful messages from family, church, or society that relate to human sexuality and the body in general.

Though the subject may be awkward for some, uncovering conflicted feelings that are entangled with a person's sense of self-confidence and identity through an open dialogue with a mature guide or counselor about one's celibacy or their sexually active life will have many benefits. Just talking openly about any previously unrecognized conflicts or feelings of shame one has regarding their body or sexuality will help calm the body and mind. Identifying any conflicts, guilt, or feelings of shame that may be present will help both the individual and their counselor determine what additional work may be needed to support that individual's chosen style of life.

Offering compassion towards your own life and towards any others you hold in important memories will also help to heal the sexual centers of the psyche and body.

It may be surprising to read comments about the need to heal any wounds that have impacted a person's sense of sexual identity in a sustained reflection on meditation and faith. Still, such comments will support the overall healing needed to aid the cultivation of faith in this way. The anger (or furious impotent rage), guilt, self-doubt, or fear that can be generated by such wounds and tangled feelings can be substantial. Healing such wounds will help the body and mind to calm and relax in ways that will support the ability to cultivate healthy experiences of friendship, love, work, and communal relations. These various efforts with memory and compassion will diminish more of the burning clusters of pain and suffering in a person's life. Those relationships, whether sexual or non-sexual, that can be healed will be more likely to be healed, or at least improved upon.

As healthier experiences of intimacy in friendship or love relations come to life, more of the tensions that had developed in the body and mind from feelings of anger, fear, and guilt will further abate. At least some experiences of peace and contentment will arise. These early intimations of well-being and liberation will inspire further willingness to explore more of what may be possible for you with personal intimacy within the bounds of the active or celibate life you feel called to.

By healing the relationship with one's self and with others, and from the resulting deepening sense of peace in silent meditation, it becomes possible to further dismantle the protective armor around the vulnerable center of the wounded self and heart. Feeling safe enough to dismantle the protective armor (or defensive shell) and to allow the wounded center to be known and experienced is a vital step. Let the wounds be known and felt for what they are, yet hold and honor them in compassionate awareness and tender care and begin to get ready to really let these wounds be healed.

As this vulnerable center is touched, enfolded, and transformed in your own compassionate care, and hopefully in the care and solicitude of sensitive friends or mentors in the present, it will be possible to perceive the more subtle realities of life. *This is because the vulnerable center of one's self and heart is one of the best channels through which the truth and deeper experience can surface into one's personal conscious experience.*

All of these various efforts will give rise to the intuitions and experiences that will allow a person to further their discernment of beliefs and values they can freely choose to have faith in.

Some will simply be able to release old feelings of anger or frustration in ways that allow them to experience a greater letting-go of self from this particular practice. Whatever path a person follows, they may notice that long overlooked experiences of guilt and shame are being seen for the first time and, over time, let go of and diffused.

Some will perceive through these channels that God is the foundation of all love and intimacy.

Some will continue to see all life as inherently impermanent and that all dharmas are empty.

Some will come to a vision of life that is different in subtle ways from either of these perspectives.

In all ways, at all times, follow your heart to see which path you are most naturally drawn to.

Follow your love and your faith in love.

17.

There are still more small steps a person can take that will help them in their search for a vision of life they can freely accept and commit to in faith before all the evidence is in.

Take the time to visit the sacred places of those faith traditions you feel called to explore.

You may or may not wish to join in the services; that is up to you.

But simply go and experience the quiet beauty and grounds of these environments by sitting silently in these sanctuaries. Take the time to notice how different are the feelings that arise when you are in such refuges as compared with other locations such as work or shopping centers you frequently visit. Take the time to notice if even in these beautiful settings you are still tense and unable to simply sit and be present.

If you do feel moved to join in with the services and sacraments that are available to you, then be as open as you can be to that which is positive and creative about the ritual and worship.

It will be helpful to try to sidestep some of the ongoing debates you have in your mind whether certain tenets of faith in different traditions are true. While these reflections are important, what may be more important is to try to get a sense of the basic intention of the creators of these special environments. Whatever serious problems may exist in any faith tradition, it is also reasonable to assume that one of the underlying intentions of these sacred places is to offer a refuge and place of consolation to all who come. Still, if you find the dysfunction of any one place or culture to be too painful and damaging for you, then it makes sense to honor the protective impulse to remove yourself from such a location.

Generally, though, whatever problems or dysfunction may be present in a particular faith tradition most churches, mosques, synagogues, monasteries, or ashrams succeed at being beautiful. Stained-glass windows, sacred architecture, chants and hymns, and sculpture are all ways to experience the sublime mystery in ways that are palpable and genuine.

Observing this art is one practice; finding ways to create sacred art and music is another highly beneficial activity. It is not that one needs to be able to rival the great artists of the past, unless one has those gifts. Rather the point being made is to find a way to create new expressions of art or crafts or simple domestic gifts. Working to create works of art or craft or beautiful gardens is a way to make something beautiful from the experiences of both joy and suffering in your life.

The creation of sacred art, chant, ritual, or craft, or making a beautiful garden give rise to experiences that help many people see through the veil of joy and sorrows to a deeper field of reality and experience. *This deeper, less visible reality may be difficult to understand rationally but is real nonetheless.* Visiting sacred places, or joining in with ancient rituals, or creating some new expression are some of the ways to explore how you can awaken experiences of intuitions of this less visible reality.

Charitable acts where you are able to offer assistance and receive the gratitude of those who are in need of kindness is another way to allow insight and experience to emerge.

Gazing silently into the eyes of your beloved as your beloved gazes back upon you is another moment for awakening. If you are able to be present with tenderness and kindness and to simply hold the one you love and be held in return, you can gaze upon and more openly receive the mysteries of mortal love.

Some may be moved to further consider how mortal love truly given and received, is somehow the mystic portal that allows you to pass to the refined and broader experience of immortal love.

Others will not.

What is true is that people of either belief system can be moved and inspired by the birth of children, the marriage rights of the betrothed, the burials of loved ones, and all the rites of passage of the different stages of life.

As people seek to experience such rites and passages openly and sensitively, any of these experiences can generate a sense of the mystery of life. When this happens, give your consent for more such experiences to arise and for the insight to explore the life behind those experiences.

From any one of these efforts, or combination of them over time, a few sparks or hints of experience and communion with life will arise from such simple but moving intentions.

Some will ask, "Who is it they have come into communion with?"

Others may not feel moved to ask this particular question.

For people following either path, the work remains to be the same. As always the way forward is to continue the search for truth and love with as much integrity, honesty, and openness as one is capable of.

Times of experience with natural beauty in the woods, or at the seashore at sunset also are evocative. The same is true of long novels about love that is gained but then lost and then at last regained at even more meaningful levels after long years of hard trials and struggle.

See what stories make you cry and weep and then ask, "Who is it you are weeping for?"

Is it not your own unmet needs for love?

Reflect on those stories of love and triumph when triumph long denied is at last denied no more.

If you are inclined to study the sacred scriptures of humanity, see if you can set aside those passages that do not speak to you so you can enjoy those beautiful or solemn passages that catch you off guard and strike a chord within. Keep on the lookout for those passages or those words or teachings you hear from others that cause you to feel in a deep way, "Yes, this really is true." When you do come across a phrase or passage that touches you deeply, spend time with that phrase or passage in a way that is called sacred reading (in the Benedictine tradition this is called Lectio Divina). This slow careful reflective reading is a way of being open to that which is sacred in the reading. When you come across a word or phrase that moves you, turn the phrase over and over in your mind. For those searching for living contact with God or spirit, after reflecting on this sacred phrase or passage you can develop a prayer of supplication based on that phrase and speak directly to the God of heaven and earth. In this prayer you can ask to be instructed in the ways of revelation and faith that are suggested or evoked by this passage. Then you can let go of the phrase and enter into silence and stillness and simply be receptive to whatever response life has to give you.

For those who seek liberation without believing in God, such patient and sincere reflection on those phrases and passages of venerable texts that are meaningful to you, will also further the journey you are on. This is because patience and sincerity and careful study of venerable literature are by themselves transformative as are the suggestions presented in earlier chapters which are now repeated.

Every single time you face up to a situation and confess that you have caused pain to someone, whether someone you know well or to a relative stranger, is another moment of great instruction.

All of us, regardless of what we believe, can feel the mystery of life surfacing within us as we finally speak the words that need to be said: "I was wrong and I will be careful not to treat you that way again." Whether others listen or accept your apology or not is not as important as the fact that you are saying to all that is holy and true in this life by your confession and atonement, "My heart is open to you. I am committed to seeing the truth about my negative tendencies. I ask to be led in the ways of grace, understanding, faith, and righteous living."

Living simply within your means and growing in kindness and integrity will also help you grow in wisdom.

Love and respect in small things, love and respect in great things, love and respect in all things will open many a mystic door to you.

By growing in wisdom you can discern more clearly what role faith, confidence, hope, and courage can play in your search for understanding, healing, and liberation. By earnestly opening your heart and mind to the truths of this life you can discern more clearly what truths, values, and living realities you can have unshakeable faith in.

You can discern more clearly how to diminish doubt, despair, alienation, and any lingering sense of hopelessness.

You can imagine what it would feel like to live without fear.

Freedom and Intimacy

Part 1

The Causes of Excessive Desire

1.

With regard to the preceding practices, each person will find their own starting point as to where it makes sense to commit their best efforts.

For some it may be high levels of anger, for others guilt, or doubt, or fear.

Others may have to find a way to work with some very tough life conditions and high levels of physical or emotional pain before much more than the basics can become possible.

For a few the fires of excessive desire might be burning so strongly that they need to do whatever they can to extinguish those fires before the house burns to the ground.

No matter where you start, the other practices need to be engaged as all these efforts complement one another. For example, a substantial portion of the turbulent emotions of anger, guilt, fear, and doubt arise from the stresses and frustrations incurred in the search to fulfill excessive desires. Therefore, as one finds healthy ways to diminish excessive desires, there simply are fewer situations where anger, guilt, fear, and doubt arise.

Conversely before one can do much about excessive desires they will need to diminish the intensity of the flames of anger, low self-esteem, and fear in their life.

It is like firefighters spraying water on different parts of a large burning house. As they make their efforts with different sides of the building, the overall fire keeps getting smaller. As they get the wider fire under control, the firefighters can combine and concentrate all their efforts on the sections of the house where the fire continues to burn.

Once the last of the visible flames are extinguished, they can then break into the walls and douse any embers smoldering in the walls or roof that could reignite the fires.

At some point even the last of the smoldering flames can be extinguished and the fire is truly out.

So it is with excessive desires and self-destructive compulsive disorders. The first efforts are to diminish any glaring forms of craving and compulsion. Then one can proceed to the ordinary desires and petty bad habits that are present in most people's lives to one degree or another. Finally one can endeavor to see and then to diminish the most subtle and covert forms of desire and self-centered preoccupations which are still quite enough to prevent the deeper experiences of peace from developing.

Still the pivotal question remains, "What are the best ways to diminish those desires and temptations that one wants and needs to forego but in the past has repeatedly given in to?"

2.

Regrettably, in many venerable commentaries or talks on liberation and craving one will often read or hear extreme statements about the need to forego all desire and forsake all attachments to all people and possessions in order to attain the higher experiences of the spiritual life.

These harsh comments have a basis in truth but they tend to confuse the issue by painting the picture with too wide a brush and too muddy a color.

Such harsh comments can discourage many from making a serious commitment to the practice of meditation and the path of liberation.

For example, some people who read or hear such teachings assume they must forego all sexual experience and let go of all forms of security and possessions as part of the process of foregoing all desire. Many quickly conclude this does not sound to be right or even possible for them and so they come to believe that silent meditation is really only for a few special people in convents, monasteries, or mountain tops.

This is not the case.

Most who seek liberation will continue to live the more ordinary life of the householder either as a single person or in the state of married life.

Some people will feel called to go further and also diminish some of the healthy and ordinary desires of the body and mind and live a celibate life in very simple living conditions alone or with other like-minded people.

For what it is worth, neither the way of the householder nor the way of the celibate renunciant is an easy path. The challenges to attaining full liberation for people leading either way of life are different but equally formidable. Still, it needs to be added that the simplified and celibate lifestyle does have the advantage of freeing up the substantial blocks of time needed for sustained practice, and this is a real benefit. Also, in a life of very simple conditions there are fewer possessions and responsibilities to look after and so it becomes far more possible to live a less stressful life.

Given that longer retreats of several weeks or months are needed for the most refined levels of concentration to develop, it is a bit hard to see how the householder can find that much dedicated time away from their other commitments. Still, a great deal of progress can be made by a diligent householder. At some point, perhaps, they can free up larger blocks of time. What is important is not to skip a brief meditation session today, just because you feel you will never have larger blocks of time for more sustained practice.

Also, some may start out on either the celibate or the householder path and realize through careful discernment that the other way of life is more appropriate for their life, temperament, and practice needs. Still, those who have generated family responsibilities before they came to such a realization need to honor the commitments they have made. For most, the day will come when those commitments will have been well met, and there will be more time for sustained study and retreats.

What is true is that people leading either way of life need to find healthy ways to diminish any and all excessive desires, compulsions, obsessions, clinging dependencies, and attachments. People leading either way of life will also need to learn to see and diminish any undertows or riptides of escapist tendencies or regressive drives to revert to a childlike state as though they no longer had adult responsibilities.

What is also true is you can learn to diminish any form of excessive desire and attachment you need to. You can even learn to restrain and then diffuse the powerful drives for sexuality and prestige if you feel called to do so, assuming you are willing to do the very basic things outlined in the second half of this chapter or in any equivalent path of study and training.

You can rely on the teaching that your experience of life and your perception of being will shift substantially when you find ways to diminish excessive desires at depth.

You can rely on the teaching that your ability to ameliorate difficult conditions in your life will be greatly enhanced by learning how to diffuse any excessive desires or compulsions that may be active.

You can rely on the teaching that your ability to diminish excessive desires will improve substantially as you learn ways to cultivate better skills with non-sexual intimacy.

3.

Still, it is much easier to talk about diminishing excessive desire than to actually do this. This is because there are many forms of excessive desire, and the causes of these differing forms of restless aching hunger are much more deeply entrenched than most are aware.

In some ways, the present age has learned much more about the root causes of many different forms of excessive desire than were known to our venerable predecessors who founded the primary monastic traditions many, many centuries ago.

These advances in knowledge and science are helpful. Knowing more about the root causes of powerful appetites will help many people to diminish more readily excessive, misguided, or openly self-destructive desires.

However inchoate the following sketches may be, and whatever corrections may be needed about certain assumptions with regard to the myriad types and causes of excessive desire, the following provides a useful overview.

4.

Some forms of excessive desire are set in motion very early in life in response to abuse or neglect or otherwise dysfunctional households. The impact of abuse, neglect, and dysfunction upon the mind of an infant or child is far-reaching. In response to such destabilizing experiences, over-compensating drives and desires may be generated as appetites for excessive security and control in ways that tend not to be present in the lives of those children who are well loved and cared for. Such over-compensations generate desires for excessive levels of security, control, and prestige, which are supposed to make up for the deprivation of love and security in infancy and youth. For example, a child who was neglected and abandoned may develop an excessive need for constant reassurance, recognition, and unrealistic levels of loyalty from people. For another, a child whose sense of self-worth was badly undermined may develop compulsive desires to attain certain achievements of prestige, status, and recognition in hopes that this external validation can shore up their shaky sense of identity and self-worth. For another, some children who grow up in chaotic households, where there was a lot of suffering and confusion, may develop very overbearing desires to control the people they are closest to. This control and rigid sense of order is a misguided effort to prevent bad things from happening. The general thought, whether consciously or unconsciously maintained, is that if people are tightly controlled then the bad kinds of volatile things that happened in youth cannot happen in adolescent or adult life. But the end result is that the people they care most about are either driven away or eviscerated of their own identity. Tragically, the end result is that a person ends up creating the very abandonment and loneliness they desperately sought to avoid. For another example, a child growing up in a household where domestic abuse was common may develop the desire to bond with an equally abusive mate in their own adult life. The presentiment develops that this is all they are worth, or this is all that life really has to offer. Again, tragically, the cycles of domestic violence are repeated and further perpetuated in the next generation.

What is particularly pernicious about these various forms of overcompensating or misguided desires is they are set in motion within a person at a very early age when the child has no chance of being consciously aware that these various forms of over-compensating drives have developed in their life. Sadly, these drives can be operative in a person's life causing painful and disruptive consequences for several decades before a person becomes mature enough to gain the awareness and insight to know how such drives have impacted their long-term choices and personality development.

The knowledge of the psychological nature of such unconsciously driven, over-compensating drives is one of the advances of the 20th century that provide a clearer conception of the origins of certain forms of excessive desire. A person can learn to become aware of such drives through various modalities of treatment such as dream therapy, behavioral change, and mindfulness training. They can then learn to diffuse these over-compensations and forms of excessive desire, although it usually takes real work over a sustained period of time to do so. Resolving very real problems and wreckage that developed in one's life as one acted upon these over-compensating desires may also be the work of years, not months, though hopefully the latter, not the former.

5.

Other forms of full-blown craving are set in motion due to compulsive self-destructive disorders such as alcoholism, addiction, excessive gambling, food disorders, promiscuity, and over-spending. These forms of craving are essentially forms of mental illness. The realization that these self-destructive compulsive disorders arise as malfunctioning brain chemistry or diseases of the organic brain rather than having been caused by sin or defilement is another advance of the 20th century. These insights provide a more accurate understanding of the root causes of many forms of compulsive disorders and extreme forms of craving.

The insights developed by the self-help groups of the 20th century to diminish these extreme forms of craving are also explored in the second half of this chapter. What is important is these same insights can be engaged by people not suffering from compulsive disorders. These insights can be engaged by those who wish and need to diminish less virulent forms of excessive desire and petty bad habits as they seek to deepen the peace of their meditations.

6.

Other forms of excessive desire are set in motion due to the impact of cynically designed mass propaganda and marketing campaigns which are designed by clever political, corporate, and militarist elites to further their unscrupulous drives for power, control, or market share.

The cravings for racial or nationalist supremacy, empire building, and the inter-ethnic hatreds brought about by such ruthless manipulations generate tremendous levels of suffering in the world. As one sees the true nature of these crude forms of craving, one can see how important it is to create cultures that emphasize the need, and that also offer the skills, to diminish such craving.

The excessive desire of powerful elites for power set in motion these manipulations that pit the people of different classes, nations, and cultures against one another. After all, if people at the bottom and middle strata of societies are hungering for revenge or war against one another, it is unlikely they will ever pose any real challenge to the cliques at the top of those societies.

Unfortunately, these kinds of manipulations are such effective techniques to accumulate political or economic power that their demise cannot be readily forecast.

The craving and hatred that arise from such manipulations can generate the most aggressive drives imaginable for revenge, massacre, religious war, racial exploitation, or even genocide and international war. The lynching of African-Americans in America, and the genocides against the Jews and Armenians of the 20th century, are graphic illustrations of the unwholesome hungers that can be unleashed in the masses by the manipulations of unscrupulous rulers.

Nothing is more tragic than the devastation wreaked by those who seek to manipulate the fear and passions of the masses as part of their drives to gratify their own selfish and misguided drives for power and other forms of accumulation and dominance.

It is an important responsibility of all citizens to see how they are in danger of being manipulated by anti-social leaders of their tribe, class, or political party. *All mature citizens need to inoculate themselves against such manipulations by cultivating the ability to think independently and to act with compassionate wisdom.* This will allow greater numbers of people not to be swept along by such manipulations of base passions and fears.

7.

Still other forms of excessive desire are set in motion from the inability or the unwillingness to see the impermanence of pleasure and all other created phenomena.

For many, when the experience of pleasure arises, the natural inclination also arises to extend that pleasure or to repeat the pleasurable experience again and again in the vain hope that such efforts can form the base of some kind of permanent happiness.

But all forms of sense pleasure are by nature impermanent. Put another way, all sense pleasures are composite phenomena. They are comprised of many parts and layers that arise from many different causes, each of which is in a state of becoming or passing away. Pleasure, like all other impermanent phenomena, will pass away since the conditions that gave rise to any particular pleasure are constantly changing. Some other impermanent experience will arise and another and another after that. Therefore it is a misguided desire to try to extend or to cling to pleasure when pleasure has begun to fade, and a suffering-generating delusion to think this is even possible. Even if you try to repeat the same pleasurable experience with the same people in the same way, the experience will be quite different.

The old quote from Heraclitus remains to be true: "The stream we dip our hand in is not the same stream we touched a moment ago."

These general explanations are a core tenet of Buddhist analysis of how the inability or unwillingness to see the impermanence of all phenomena is a root cause that gives rise to misguided desires and suffering. This important subject is explored in greater detail in the last chapter entitled "Illusion and Insight."

8.

As powerful as these various causes and forms of excessive desire are, there are other forms of blind striving and wanting that are even more powerful.

The most powerful drives of desire for the vast majority of people are set in motion by the force of genetically-transmitted and biochemically-triggered instinctual drives and appetites. Some of these instinctual programs of behavior and hunger we humans inherited from earlier species; some are unique to human evolution. The insights that many ordinary and excessive desires arise from instinctual forms of appetite are additional important examples of the advances of the current age. The discoveries that such instinctual appetites are genetically transmitted and biochemically triggered are important enhancements to the traditional analysis of the causes of desire such as the ones depicted in the previous sections.

Chief among these instinctual desires are: the drive to survive, the drive for procreation and sexual experience, the drive to battle for territory especially among males, the drive to hunt, the drive to build shelter, the need for love, the drive to give special care to our loved ones, and the drive for rank or dominance within the social group.

The power of these drives and the substantial efforts expended to gratify these instinctual desires constitute the vast majority of all human desire, activity, struggle, and effort.

The impact of the instincts is profound, especially when one considers what happens when instincts are combined with the power and the aptitudes of the human brain.

The instincts combine with the unique aptitudes of human memory and language to create the formation of the voice of self and ego that is the voice within that says "I" and "me" and "I hunger" and "I thirst."

Over countless eons and many life forms, the evolutionary process generated what we call the self, or personal consciousness, as a new agent equipped with new skills to coordinate the choices and actions required to try to gratify the instinctual desires.

The needs, deeply felt by many to gratify the imperatives of the ego, are additional spurs to ensure the likelihood that the instinctual drives will be gratified for such goals as achieving a higher rank within the tribe or the seduction of high-status sexual partners.

The ego gratifications that arise from victory in competitive struggles or the feelings of the surge of power at the attainment of high rank within the social group are additional biochemical carrots and reward mechanisms. These special kinds of gratification experiences serve as a reward function to give people extra motivation to try to win whatever it is we are being manipulated to try to win by our biology.

Tragically, most of us are not even aware we are being drawn to make many of the most persistent efforts of our life only because of biochemical manipulations developed in the random course of evolution.

Adding further charge and texture to this already intricate biochemical matrix has been the evolution over many tens of millions of years of the sensors and the sensations of pleasure and pain. The development of these sensors and sensations of pleasure and pain through the evolutionary process is another foundational layer of the animal and human nervous system that has had incalculable impact.

The sensors and the sensations of pleasure and pain, and the way these sensors are deeply intertwined with important centers of the brain, greatly reinforce the voice of "I" and "me" and "mine."

The hope and the deeply-felt needs for sensual and emotional pleasure are the carrots generated by evolution to seek to compel the individual to make the efforts needed to gratify the instinctual desires. The stings of physical and emotional pain are the sharp sticks or whips generated by the evolution of complex nervous systems. Both these lures and drivers function like spurs digging in and pushing us to take immediate and extensive actions to gratify instinctual desires, thereby feeling the pleasure, thereby making the pain stop.

The force of instinct and the imperatives to gratify instinct, coupled with the hope of pleasure, or the digging spurs of pain, or the fear of pain, all combine to create most of what we call the self and ego and our experience of life.

"I want this sensation," "I want more of this sensation," "I want this sensation to last."

"I don't like this pain or deprivation." "I fear the pain I will feel if I don't do certain things."

It is not clear how many millions of years were needed for language and memory to develop to the point where the voice formed within that says, "I hunger" and "I thirst," " I need," "I want," "I will look for" and "I will just take what I want" but these developments did happen. The layers of reason, feeling, and complexity of modern consciousness which were added as overlays to this instinctual and sensorial core began to develop several thousand years ago and accelerated tremendously in the past five centuries.

The impact of the formation of the self and the ego along with the development of pleasure as the carrot and pain as the stick of interior experience, coupled with the aptitudes of language, concept formation, and memory is tremendous. The force and blare of instinct, coupled with the other forms of desire and the carrot and stick of pleasure and pain, ego gratification or ego humiliations, coupled with the general force and aptitudes of personal consciousness we call the "self" creates a formidable matrix of inner forces.

It is this powerful matrix of inner forces that the contemplative person tries to ameliorate with practices such as the ones in this commentary of the simple path and other commentaries or "paths of purification."

Before proceeding, it is important to add that none of these comments about the force and impact of genetically-based and biochemically-triggered instinctual desires is to imply that we are little more than robots, although sadly most people do not ever become much more.

What is being said is that we are not born with a clean slate; far from it.

What is also being said is that it is important to better understand the origin and nature of the ordinary and excessive desires of your life and the full impact of these forms of "wanting."

What is important is to see as much of this as you can so you are at least not surprised at how difficult the journey can be at times.

After all, knowing the true root causes of ordinary and excessive desires will help develop the understanding needed to diminish those desires that are impediments to the cultivation of deeper experiences of peace and clarity.

After all, once you realize that most of the important goals and efforts of your life are not even ones you have chosen, but which you were driven to seek by the triggers of biology, you may begin to reassess what it is you really do want in this life.

What is also important is to be fully aware of the spectrum and force of excessive desires so that you can gain a full appreciation for the level of effort, courage, and diligence needed to quiet the sources of stress and restless aching hunger within.

9.

Look closely at the various forms and efforts related to ordinary and excessive desire and the arising, peaking, and passing away of all desires.

This detailed effort of observation is another way to build up the stamina and continuity of one's ability to be mindfully aware of each moment.

There are the instinctual desires.

There are the distorted needs for security, control, and prestige that arise for many as psychological compensations for deprivation, abuse, or abandonment.

There are the drives and desires inculcated by family, social expectations, and competitive jostling among peers in the tribe.

For most, there are also at least a few petty desires or bad habits that are surprisingly difficult to break.

For others, there are deeply embedded compulsive disorders for stimulants, food, gambling, promiscuity, and the like, which can develop into a full-blown struggle for survival.

There the petty ambitions of self and ego and for some the overt hungers for power and domination generated by extreme forms of selfish delusion.

There are the drives to gratify pleasure. There are the experiences of gratifying those desires. There is the passing of the experience of gratification into some other experiences. There is the desire to prolong pleasure even though it is clear the moment of pleasure is passing or has already fled.

There are the efforts to understand which desires are permissible to gratify and which are not.

There are also the inner battles whether to resist or to give in to what are deemed to be illicit or illegal desires. If one gives into illicit hungers or criminal desires there are the experiences that arise from the decision to break the rules and gratify these forbidden wants and forms of hunger. There are the experiences of guilt, shame, or remorse in many people once the illicit, unhealthy, or sadistic desires have been gratified and are now past. Then there are the consequences of giving into illicit desires. In cases where a person gives into temptations to commit serious breaches of the moral code such as acts of adultery, criminal behavior, or blind aggression the consequences can be very serious and even life changing.

For those given to art, ideas, and science, there is the hunger for glory and recognition for having made some breakthrough discovery in the chosen field.

For those given to sport or war, there are the hungers for victory, the fears of defeat, the efforts to be victorious or the efforts to endure what is perceived to be the shame and humiliation of defeat and ignominy.

For many, there are the attachments to certain people that the self feels are needed as foundations of identity and security as though one particular lover is the only one that can complete a person's inner experience and serve as the foundation of lasting happiness.

There are the unconscious drives that emerge in dreams and in unexpected slips of tongue, the so-called Freudian slips. There are the repressed desires that one is unable to gratify or which one feels would be wrong or dangerous to gratify which still fester and smolder beneath the threshold of awareness.

The purpose of this long list is to elucidate some of the vast amount of activity which occurs in the relatively small organ we call the brain.

Just seeing how complex is the web of ordinary and excessive desire and the related efforts and conflicts of desire is an important insight. One can begin to see the full force and power of what we vaguely refer to as the self, and all the desires that arise from what we call the self, or personal consciousness, and ego.

The sense of self and ego, of "I" and "me" and "I want" and "I don't want" can be so strong and glaring it is often difficult to realize how much of an impact they have on our experience of our own life in particular and how we view the rest of life in general.

The experience of a life dominated by the force and blare of self and ego can be likened to that of a person living in a world where the sun never sets. If a person lives in such a world, they may live their whole life without ever seeing the beauty of the endless night sky that becomes visible when the sun has set. If a person lives in a world where the sun never sets, their universe will seem to be very small. If the sun never sets they will never gain the chance to see hundreds of millions of galaxies sprawled across far flung reaches of space and time beyond their own small world.

There needs to be a way for this life-giving but glaring sun to set.

The questions remain:

> "How can one find the resources needed not to give into temptations and desires that one clearly feels are unskillful, or openly immoral, which one has repeatedly given into in the past?"

> "How can one diminish the underlying causes of excessive desires and those ordinary desires one chooses to forego so that these urges and desires do not arise in the first place?"

The challenge also remains:

> "How can one honor the difficulties they experience as they make a serious effort to diffuse old habits of excessive desire, compulsion, or obsession?"

Freedom and Intimacy

Part 2

Skillful Means to Diminish Excessive Desire

12.

It is important not to be too discouraged by the formidable array of internal drivers of excessive desire listed in the first half of this chapter. This is easier said than done as these drives are often much stronger than the powers of restraint available to us as individuals.

The reason for hope arises from the simple fact that, as powerful as all these forms of genetics, biology, psychology, and craving are, there are other currents of life that are even more powerful and elemental. These deeper and more subtle currents and fields of life and energy are capable of diffusing and washing away even the most virulent drivers of craving, restless aching hunger, and blind striving.

These deeper aquifers and currents of life are called grace or spirit, as alluded to in the chapter entitled "Confession and Grace," at least in some traditions.

If you feel a different terminology is more consistent with your path or tradition, then use that terminology or develop your own.

What is important is to realize that this grace, or energy, is a real resource embedded in the mind, heart, and blood of every person. The simple proof of this is to observe the special quality of the feelings which arise when you freely admit faults and make genuine efforts to correct faults.

If you want to know what grace is, observe closely the feelings which arise when, instead of telling old lies about some important situation, you finally commit to telling the whole truth, and nothing but the truth.

Observe the feelings that arise when you get honest about any mean and petty things you have done that are hurtful to others which previously you refused to admit. Observe the feelings that arise when others truly forgive you for actions you had done which hurt them very much. Observe the feelings that arise when you are able to forgive those who have done serious wrong to you even if they took no real notice of your generous act of forgiveness.

Look carefully at the feelings that arise when you read a story about a man or woman who had been a terrible criminal who has made very genuine changes in their life and is now living a life of dedicated service to others.

Grace is present in all people at all times but generally only surfaces into consciousness when real commitments to grow in love and moral character are made by an individual. Each individual can decide to make this commitment. It is the choice to make or not make this commitment that provides the clearest context where the truth and beauty of the doctrine of free will can be seen most clearly. However limited the doctrine of free will may be as a response to other serious questions about human suffering and the origins of evil, in this context the doctrine is completely true.

Many believe that the grace of love and the desire to mature in moral nature are the only forces known to be strong enough to transform the underlying rip tides of excessive desire, aggression, and clinging attachment. Those who tend to believe in this way also believe that only God as the source of grace is powerful enough to transform human nature into the likeness of the divine. Those who do not believe in God have other ways to understand and describe the functions of grace or what they may call the general favorable encouragement of life, or more simply, "going with the flow."

For example, from the atheist tradition of Theravada Buddhism we find such general phenomena described in this way by two contemporary writers, "When you surrender the stance of personal control, you invite a greater, more universal aspect to join in the process."[5]

To be fair, many conservative Theravada Buddhists, and others, may challenge the above comment as being an ill-considered revisionist view of their tradition. After all, there is no need to ascribe to Theravada Buddhism certain teachings that really do not reflect historical consensus. Should some Buddhists come to believe there is a "universal aspect" to life which comes to the aid of people renouncing self-centered living, it is enough to be clear they are engaging a further development of their tradition. This approach would be more respectful to those who adhere to the old ways rather than saying that such ideas were taught indirectly in their tradition all along. What is significant about the above comment of these well respected teachers is that it illustrates the general idea of "grace" or "universal aspect" is one which circulates widely through many spiritual cultures. That this is true *even, at times, in those cultures which appear, or purport to be, atheist traditions* may be especially worthy of note to any whose search for truth is genuinely unbiased.

Still it is a very fair question to ask where or how this grace or energy may be embedded in the foundations of our heart, mind, and body. While the following suggested lines of inquiry are highly

5   Stephen Snyder and Tina Rasmussen, *Practicing the Jhanas*. Boston: Shambala Publications, 2009, p. 65.

speculative, they are still worthy of exploration. The terms "grace" or "holy spirit" may be, at bottom, ways to describe certain attributes of energy, the energy which is the foundation of all matter. As modern physicists have learned, energy and matter are two sides of the same coin. What has not been given as much attention by spiritual or scientific people are the questions related to the actual nature and attributes of that which we refer to as energy or light.

We have become skilled at measuring energy, and using energy in countless technological applications. But we do not really know much about the nature or true life of energy. It is offered for consideration that the exploration into the true nature and attributes of energy is an important frontier for spiritual and scientific inquiry. The same can be said for the exploration into the true nature and attributes of consciousness. Modern neuroscientists have begun the effort to better understand and chart the phenomena of human consciousness. But we are still years and possibly decades away from any definitive answers that qualify as objective knowledge. What is clear is that wherever consciousness is present, energy is also present. The question can fairly be asked, "Is it also true that wherever energy is present that consciousness is also present?"

This is not to propose that all energy is conscious in the way we think of humans as being conscious. It is just that as our definitions of the words "consciousness" and "life" are continuing to evolve, and we do not know how much further these definitions may expand. Forms of life have been discovered in the past few decades that were not thought possible under the standard definitions of what life was thought to be and what conditions were needed for life to exist. As these definitions of life and consciousness continue to evolve, we may yet find some unexpected answers. We may find that the energy that permeates the universe is actually a form of life and consciousness. We may find that the universe is itself some form of life or mind as many of the ancients suggested with terms such as "nous," "logos," "divine consciousness," "Brahman," or "Buddha nature." We may find that this universal life is somehow alive and has an experience of being alive. In short the infinite universe may have an experience of being infinite that overlaps, or supersedes our experience of being finite. We may find that the universe is a vast ocean of divine consciousness and realms of being.

We may find that what we think of as grace is a way to describe the special attributes of energy and consciousness. If what we refer to as grace is actually a description of some of the properties of energy and consciousness then this would explain how and where grace may be embedded in the firmament of our lives. Energy and grace may be the life of the atoms and cells of our body, and the atoms of all material reality. Energy and grace may be the base stratum and element of the feelings and thoughts of our mind.

If energy permeates the universe, and if energy is somehow a form of grace and consciousness, then this may provide answers to the great question as to whether God does or does not exist. Whether we are willing to believe in God or not, the fact may emerge that the universe is a living conscious being, however different this infinite consciousness may be compared to our ordinary living and waking consciousness. We may find that the refined states that arise from a sophisticated cultivation of meditation are somehow more closely analogous to the nature of universal consciousness than are the tones of more ordinary waking awareness and thought. This is said, again, with the caveat that the nature of this infinite consciousness is likely very, very different from anything we generally think of as our ordinary, decision-making, human awareness.

However speculative such propositions may be, and however much refinement may be needed over time to these core insights, they may yet help us in many ways. We may yet learn to more effectively draw upon these aquifers of energy, grace, and life within us in ways that will support the general process of discovering new ways to heal physical and mental illness. We may yet learn important new ways to draw upon these pools of life within us in ways that help us more readily override the forces of instinct and excessive desire within us. We may yet learn important ways to draw upon these aquifers within us to more expeditiously awaken the illumination of mind and spirit that prophets, seers, and saints have told of down through the ages. Why is the search for liberation often so long and arduous? Are there ways this search can be greatly simplified so that more can find their way, more quickly and directly to the lakes of heaven within?

How is it that the greatest teachers and saints have found ways to complete great undertakings with almost no resources other than their personal faith, insight, life, and example? How is it that the greatest teachers and saints have been able to endure trials that would have broken many others, and to inspire countless millions down through the ages?

The story of the former prince meditating in the forests of Nepal twenty five centuries ago comes to mind. The story of the carpenter dying alone in disgrace on a cross twenty centuries ago comes to mind. The story of the caravan merchant in Arabia fighting for his life and the life of his followers in a remote outpost outside of Mecca comes to mind. The story of Mother Teresa leaving her convent with no money and no followers and creating with a few decades a worldwide religious order and charitable enterprise is another great example of this unique phenomena. The story of a handful of low bottom alcoholics coming together and then discerning a treatment for alcoholism that was missed by the best educated specialists in the field is also evocative of the deeper processes of life that we do not fully understand.

What is this grace and feeling that we feel surfacing in our life when we engage the practices of confession and atonement? How much further can we cultivate the resources of empathy and the sense of connection we experience when we take the steps needed to heal primary relationships that had been badly damaged by our former acts?

What is it within us that responds so deeply when we encounter someone who is truly holy and very kind regardless of their particular spiritual tradition or cultural orientation.

However described or left undescribed, the efficacy of grace is very real regardless of how different people relate to or understand this particular force of psyche and nature. A sincere and consistent practice of confession, remorse, and atonement will confirm this truth to anyone. This confirmation will be known from the unique tone and "feel" of the personal, subjective experiences which arise as a person engages these practices. Additional confirmation of this truth will be known from the significant enhancements which accrue in the viable relationships of a person's life as they engage these efforts with a genuinely earnest commitment.

This grace, which inspires and enables people to heal their existing relationships will also help them to cultivate better skills with non-sexual intimacy. *Experiences of non-sexual intimacy will help to deepen the sense of intuition that serves as the basis for faith, and the experiences of communion.* Such experiences will also help diffuse the neural clusters that form the rigid edges of self, ego, and instinct and any deeply anti-social behaviors that may be present in a person's life.

But what really is non-sexual intimacy?

Non-sexual intimacy arises when we are accepted and affirmed by another as being valuable even if there is still a lot of personal work we need to do to be a more complete, morally mature and compassionate person.

Non-sexual intimacy arises when people can be who they are with one another, within the reasonable boundaries of tolerance and diversity, without shame or self-conscious censoring or repression or fear of damage.

Non-sexual intimacy arises when people can talk about serious problems and issues they are having in their life without being afraid of being judged, belittled, rejected, or ostracized for having the problems they have.

Non-sexual intimacy arises when people can laugh and have good times and fellowship with one another as ordinary moments are shared and important passages of life are celebrated. This sense of well-being arises when people are able to trust one another and when they can get together to play in light-hearted games and have fun and laughs.

Non-sexual intimacy arises when a person realizes they are loved as they are by one who has no other agenda than to love them with grace and skill.

13.

The instincts to survive, to have sex and procreate, the instinct for rank in the group, the battles for territory, to hunt, to build shelter, and care for loved ones and members of one's clan are not the only instincts of humans.

At least for many people, perhaps for all, the mind and heart also have a fundamental need for non-sexual intimacy, relationality, and empathy. It is possible that the emotion of love is nothing more than another adaptive trait developed in the evolutionary process to further the instincts of procreation and the defense and maintenance of families, tribes, and individuals. *But love seems and feels to be something more than this.*

Love and the need for love may be born from an intuition of the benevolent life that is embedded in the very depths of who we are and in the depths of all being.

The experience of healthy relationality meets some very basic needs of the psyche in the same way sunlight, rain, and good soil meet the very basic needs of plants and trees.

These experiences of well-being that arise from healthy fellowship are the factors that allow the celibate person to diffuse the powerful drives for sexual experience and need for high social rank. It is these experiences that allow a person to settle into a viable celibacy and simple life, should they feel called to such a way of life.

Experiences of non-sexual intimacy also enable and inspire sexually active persons to remain faithful to their beloved instead of going where their wandering eye and appetites at times urge them to go. *High-grade skills with non-sexual intimacy will also help a sexually active couple keep their relationship growing after mere passion fades, as all mere passion will.*

Better skills with non-sexual intimacy will also heighten the beauty and pleasure of sexual intimacy for those who have chosen to live in a healthy, which is to say a committed, relationship.

So much of the work of the simple path is to find ways to enhance the quality of all of one's relationships.

As healthier relationships become possible, love, intimacy, and well-being arise.

This love, intimacy, and well-being help reduce feelings of isolation, alienation, fear, and worthlessness. These positive experiences of intimacy also help diffuse misguided notions of inferiority and superiority, all of which can sharply inflame and distort those forms of desire generated by biological instinct.

Tapping into the reservoirs of grace that are embedded in the fundamental stratum of our life through the practices of confession, compassion, and faith will allow the most creative energies of the psyche to circulate.

Grace, as it circulates freely and openly throughout the psyche, transforms all it washes through.

As the needs of the psyche for love, intimacy, and well-being are met, the underlying causes of excessive desire, craving, and delusion subside and the mind can quiet further.

Fear subsides and it is more possible to really "let go" at a deeper level.

None of this is to imply there is some effortless way to diminish deeply-rooted patterns of excessive desire, self-destructive drives, compulsion, obsession, clinging attachment, misguided emotional dependencies, escapist behavior, or magical thinking.

None of this is to imply that there is some easy way to resist regressive desires, which can be defined as desires to revert to the state of infancy we all began with where someone took care of, or was supposed to take care of, all of your needs.

What is being said is that there is a way to diffuse the formidable drives and impulses of excessive desires in ways that lead to the deepest states of peace, clarity, and concentration.

What is also being said is that serious and sustained efforts and moral reform and renewal, along with experiences of non-sexual intimacy, will awaken the deeper powers of life and psyche. Allowing the deeper currents of psyche and being to surface into the unconscious and conscious strata of the mind will help diffuse the various conflicted drives of full-blown, restless aching hunger and craving so that more joy can arise.

14.

What is essential is this:

> For many it will prove to be important to realize that one's personal will-power and discipline alone may not be enough to restrain excessive desire and powerful unwanted temptations.

For many people, the best-known way to diminish any unwanted temptations and excessive desire is to seek healthy relations with other people who have already learned how to diminish the specific desires you are still struggling with.

It is possible to go further with this observation.

For some people the <u>only</u> way to diminish excessive desire and self-destructive tendencies is to form healthy relationships with mature people so they can benefit from the help, positive example, connection, and guidance which mature people have to offer. *For such people the exertions of will-power are no more helpful than trying to put out a fire by pouring gasoline on it.*

Grace is the subtle, streaming energy that is released between two people when a healthy sense of non-sexual intimacy, honesty, and acceptance is the living field of that relationship.

The lessons learned from self-help groups about the role that a tolerant, open-minded, but highly dedicated spirituality can play in diminishing powerful forms of craving are some of the most important empirical evidence available to humanity. The lessons learned from these self-help groups provide valuable insights into how the right approach to personal and communal relationships and the right context of belief can help diminish excessive desire.

If you know some other ways to diminish excessive desire that work better for you, then engage those other ways.

If nothing else you have tried is effective at helping you to diminish excessive desire, then try the following suggestions.

15.

The first key to this process is to find people who are committed to high-integrity living. It is best to look for people who have made serious commitments to spiritual, or at least highly ethical, values. The other critical aspect of the people you are looking for is that they are mature enough not to need you to agree with their particular views, unless you naturally share their beliefs. Look for people who will encourage you to understand the need to make a very serious effort to find ethical and spiritual values that work for you, even if your views and vision of life differ from theirs.

The second key to this process is to find people who will not judge you for the excessive desires and temptations you are struggling with, but who will validate your experience and emotions as you consider the changes you need to make in your life.

An important part of all this is the work previously highlighted in earlier chapters to reduce strong feelings of anger, guilt, fear, and doubt.

One of the reasons so much emphasis has been placed on these efforts is that they are necessary to form the healthier relationships that allow grace to circulate more freely between people and within each person. It is this freer circulation of grace that is needed to diminish excessive desire.

As anger, guilt, and fear subside, you will be well on your way to heal the relationship you have with yourself and with those people in your personal life and work-related activities. As faith and skill arise, it will also be possible to heal or clarify your relationship with the broader spirit or currents of life. All of these relationships need to be in the best condition that is reasonably possible in order to do the work of diminishing excessive desire.

What the self-help groups of the 20th and 21st centuries have demonstrated is that a high degree of sustained immersion into the life of a healthy group of people can be an effective aid in diffusing sharp craving. This note is offered with the additional comments that sincere efforts at moral renewal and at least a general but sincere openness to faith in love, honesty, forgiveness, and service are other critically important aspects of this method.

The essential thinking is this: As urges, impulses, and temptations arise on a very habitual basis throughout the day and week, then emotionally healthy involvement with mature people is also needed throughout the day and week as a steady countermand to urge and impulse.

During high tides of desire, stress, and restless aching hunger, the engagement with healthy friends or mentors may need to be almost constant throughout the day and night until the tides recede.

Remember, all desires, stresses, and restless aching hungers are composite experiences. Remember, all composite experiences are by nature impermanent and will pass.

Therefore any excessive desire will pass away sooner or later if you can just get through the high tides of urge and craving. At some point a person can learn how to diffuse the underlying causes at depth so that the urges do not arise in the first place. But for now it is enough for a person to seek the help of other mature people to be with as they wait out the high tides of self-destructive craving. Countless incidents of healthy engagement with others during high tides of desire have provided empirical proof that such engagement is an efficacious means to diminish craving. The challenge is to find enough mature people for a support network so that no one person is overloaded, or in case any one person simply exits the support network.

Only with a fairly broad network of sustaining relationships will it be possible to have access to enough people able and willing to help you divert your attention from, or simply wait out, the high tides of excessive desires till they break apart and fade, which being impermanent they will.

Other final elements of this method are that such groups or networks of support need to be fundamentally non-hierarchical. The only genuine authority being, at least, a general sense of more broadly compassionate life as manifested in the positive intentions and example of seasoned and experienced members. Very real commitments to keep the material possessions and organizational structure of the group as simple as possible are other important traits.

As needed, during high and low tides of excessive desire, members call upon one another and their "higher power" in trust and faith. This helps urges to pass and weaken, and as they pass and weaken they become less frequent over time. The caveat being that each person is free to develop their own vision of what that higher power may be, although it is strongly suggested that one gravitate to a sense of a "greater power" that is benevolent and supportive.

It is the safety, non-judgmental, and non-hierarchical nature of these relationships that gives rise to experiences of non-sexual intimacy. It is this felt sense of intimacy which is able to induce or evoke experiences of well-being, connection, and a greater sense of freedom.

It is these experiences of well-being and personal connection to healthy mature people, as well as laughter and simple good times in a morally clear setting, that are enough to wash away the drivers of excessive desire, anger, fear, and restless aching hunger.

The same process also works to diminish petty escapist desires and bad habits.

The general challenge is that petty escapist desires and bad habits are not life-threatening and so the sense of urgency does not exist to make the same degree of effort to diminish these levels of desire. Sadly, these petty escapist desires and bad habits are enough to disrupt one's effort to cultivate the best quality skills with, and the most pure experiences of, mindful awareness and single point concentration.

There is an important caveat to these general remarks. Sadly, there are many people who do not find effective healing from this general process and never really are able to diminish their self-destructive craving. *Why this process works well for many and not for many others is another very interesting research theme of our times.*

What is important is this method of immersion into the life of healthy groups has represented the single greatest step forward in the treatment of alcoholism and addiction and many other forms of compulsive self-destructive craving. With care and reflection it should be possible to learn how to refine this process so it works for greater percentages of people attracted to this healing modality.

16.

Still, an ongoing problem for quite a few people is that it is difficult for them to find healthy groups or communities of like-minded people they can join.

This is especially true if a person does not naturally and freely fit into any of the molds generally required for organized religion or some other spiritual group.

Another lesson that can be learned from the self-help groups is by noting how willingly they accept newcomers that others communities might not wish to bother with.

What is important is to keep looking for groups that you can join, at least as a peripheral member, and gain the benefits of that partial level of acceptance, fellowship, and involvement.

The more serious the degree of excessive desire or compulsion you are experiencing, the more important it is to join in as best you can with the mature groups you are able to find. Even a limited involvement will help you to break out of any tendencies towards isolation that may be damaging your overall efforts. Over time you may see a clear path for more involvement with one of the groups you have been attending.

The key is to look for groups of people where at least some of the members have already found a way to diminish the excessive desires you are struggling with.

What is also important is to keep doing the basic work of meditation, concentration, compassion, confession, and faith in the context of those values that you are able to embrace as you continue your search for truth and healing.

For as you heal from within, you will be better able to form healthier relationships with others and to make allowances for the limitations of people and groups you encounter.

As you heal from within, you will be better able to see in what ways you are contributing to whatever general problems with relationships and non-sexual intimacy you are experiencing.

Also, as you heal by stages from within you will tend to meet healthier friends and mentors. Why this last point is true may not be known exactly, but this general tendency does seem to be the case. You can rest assured that as you embrace higher standards of sincerity, honesty, decency, and compassion, you will find other skillful, intelligent, and mature people sooner or later.

Over time you will find at least a few people with whom you can have sustaining relationships wherein you both can grow in skill to diminish excessive desire, unwanted temptations, and misguided hungers. Over time you will also become more independent and able to persevere on your own if you need to. You may not be able to find any one group or community that really is a match, but it may be very possible to be part of several different groups, each of which has enough partial benefits to sustain you until a more optimal match may be found.

Do not run away if there are some difficult experiences with people in a given group as long as those clashes are not too severe. One of the real benefits of group involvement is that the personality clashes you stumble or blunder into will bring to the surface a wide variety of those fears, emotions, and personality traits you need to work on. However, if a group of people simply is not healthy, or there really is not enough of a match, that is a different matter. You may well need to withdraw from any active involvement with them.

But the clashes and disagreements that arise from relationships can be some of the best learning experiences for you. It seems, to a degree, many of us learn our most important lessons through conflict and skillful resolution of conflict. Over time, as one becomes more conscious and skillful, proactive choices for growth that do not involve so much storm and stress become possible. Unfortunately, a general problem in community life is that so few groups and communities have any real skill with allowing conflict within the group to surface and to process that conflict in creative and effective ways. The paucity of this skill within most groups makes participation in community life more difficult for the individual members of those groups, especially for people who really do have a lot to learn about basic emotional intelligence.

If by temperament or character flaw you tend to be immature, socially awkward, abrasive, or disruptive, then there simply will be fewer groups of people willing to do the work of accepting you into the normal life of their group. If this is the case, then do not judge yourself too harshly. It is enough simply to keep looking for those groups who may be more flexible and mature, and continue to work on any anti-social traits of yours that really may be getting in the way.

However, if you are afflicted with compulsive self-destructive disorders such as addiction, gambling, eating disorders, serial promiscuity, workaholic tendencies, criminality, self-cutting, degraded sexual practices, or the like, then seek whatever help is available immediately.

It is important to put out any fires burning in your house before the house burns to the ground.

Depending on how deeply embedded such afflictions or habit patterns may be in your life, it may be a difficult and protracted struggle to diminish such powerful forms of craving.

What is important is that it is possible to diminish even full-blown obsession and craving.

What is important is to seek the best help you can find as quickly as you can.

What is important is to be open-minded enough to make sure you are not rejecting good assistance simply because you are being asked to face and change old forms of behaviors and attitudes.

Even if the help you find is less than perfect, try to make the best use of it you can and keep searching for better help and never, never, never give up.

What can any of us do but begin, or begin again where we are?

Remember, whenever you are confused you can always seek to better learn to be as gentle with yourself and with others as you can be and to keep searching for the "next right thing to do."

17.

The first threshold of freedom is to clear the body of any and all stimulants as you prepare for times of silent meditation.

The second threshold of freedom is to simplify your life and ambitions to the degree that you have good quality time for daily practice of silent meditation and that you maintain this daily practice.

The third threshold of freedom is to find healthy ways to simplify your diet so that the abdomen is as light and clear as health will allow as you prepare for times of silence and stillness.

The fourth threshold of freedom is to clear the mind of angry thoughts of aggression and revenge along with the other turbulent emotions of fear, doubt, guilt, vanity, and the like.

The fifth threshold of freedom is to be willing to let go of all the plans, schemes, agendas of self, whether they are petty or noble, except for the general plan to continue to seek liberation.

The sixth threshold of freedom is to be willing to let go of the needs and cares of all other people, regardless of whether those needs are valid or not, during times of formal meditation practice that are not dedicated to affirmation practice.

The seventh threshold of freedom is to let go of any unconfident and over-confident images of self as well as any descriptions that describe the self one way or the other.

As you begin this process, what is important is to diminish the most destructive and crudest forms of craving in your life so that you can then endeavor to reduce the remaining petty bad habits and dependencies. For many this work is slow and definitely of a two-step-forward, one-step-backward, two-step-forward, one-step-backward nature. But then the day comes when it is two-steps-forward and one-step-backward, and then three-steps-forward and only one-step-backward.

Be as patient as you can be with any setbacks and disappointments you experience with your hopes of becoming free, really free.

Be patient, but work as diligently as you reasonably can.

Continue to seek the best help and guidance you can find.

Continue to make the best use of that help and guidance you do encounter that seems real and true, even if you are not sure how to put the offered suggestions into actual practice.

See if someday you can become the clear and trustworthy friend or elder who is able to give to others the very help and insight that you once needed but which was not available to you at earlier times in your struggle and journey.

18.

There is something that can be done by those who believe in God, or who are willing to try to believe in God. They can call upon God in hope and trust for guidance and help to diminish unwanted cravings, urges, and bad habits. The act of calling out to God is a way of declaring a further opening and consent to grace, and such declaration is another way to allow more grace to circulate more freely throughout your life.

An ever deeper surrender in faith, trust, acceptance, and passive receiving of grace will continue to provide better and better sustaining life and inspiration. While each individual will need to continue to labor and to continue to choose to do "the next right thing," God's grace and care will help you discern "the next right thing to do."

The further cultivation of high-grade skills of awareness, concentration, and compassion continue to be of primary benefit. One needs to be able to observe deeply and clearly in order to see desires arise, to understand the true source of desires and to cultivate concentration to the point where it is possible to make choices about which desires are healthy and which desires need to be diffused.

The practices of confession and making amends for any and all harm caused to others or to one's self continue to be the single most essential way to open the channels of grace within you needed to diminish the underlying causes of excessive desire and petty bad habits. Anyone who is not willing and able to be rigorously honest with themselves and other people and with God, if they have chosen a God-centered path, will find it very difficult to outgrow the habit patterns of excessive desire, clinging, dependency, and attachment.

If you do not believe in God, then you will need to find some other source of power that will help you diffuse those forms of excessive desire and ordinary desire you feel called to forego. The important general guideline that is suggested is to find something other than your own personal self to which you can open your heart and mind for guidance and sustenance. For many who seek liberation without a belief in God, they find the fellowship of their friends and mentors and the venerable texts of their tradition to be sufficient sources they can turn to for help.

It is the realization that you can find healthy guidance and support from others, and a willingness to listen to the healthy guidance of others and to receive that support they are willing to give to you that is important.

If you have no interest in God or spirit that is your choice.

But a healthy community of people, along with the teachers and teachings of that community are enough to form the base of a "higher power" that can help you diffuse the raw aching hunger and the gross or petty escapist desires you are prone to. Some may wish to argue that this community and set of teachings is God's presence even though the people involved do not wish to use this word. Some may continue to insist that a community and positive set of teachings are purely human creations and there is no divine spirit as the base of that community or teachings.

Some may wish to argue for one point or another, but who really cares?

Find out what works for you.

Find out what helps you enhance the quality of love, respect, and friendship you have to offer.

Find out what helps you experience the greatest degree of true freedom.

You may wish to call the assistance you receive God, or Goddess, or the Law, or Dharma, that is up to you.

The only caveat to this very broad-minded approach is this: should you be experiencing life-threatening levels of self-destructive desires and disorders, then do not wait for subtle reflection. Simply call out as you would if someone was attacking you on a dark, lonely street.

"Help!" "Someone help me."

Or, "God help me."

For it is rightly said, "A short prayer pierces the heavens."[6]

6   *Cloud of Unknowing* Chapter 37.

Humility and Vanity

1.

The analysis of the myriad causes of desire illustrates how much force and blare exist in what we vaguely refer to as the self and the entire range of interior drives and impulses.

The earlier efforts to diminish anger, guilt, fear, and doubt will all help to quiet the force and blare of these inner dynamics.

The work to diminish excessive desires and any levels of compulsion that are present, is further essential work which supports this overall effort. The general direction of all these practices is to diminish by stages the general force of stress in the mind and heart.

It is like a person who has begun their search by waking up from a deep sleep which is troubled by many dreams who upon awakening finds there is a hurricane blowing at full force in their town.

As the day proceeds, the hurricane moves over land and the velocity of the winds of the storm begins to taper down. First the hurricane is downgraded from a category four or five hurricane to a category two or three. Then, in another day or two, the hurricane is further downgraded to a tropical storm, and from there to gale force winds.

At some point the storm is simply gone.

The work with humility suggested in this chapter will further diminish the storm clouds and howling winds of self-centered preoccupations that lead to suffering. The cultivation of humility will let the air out of any vain, puffed up, clamoring aspects of self that may still be active in your life.

By degree, the mind will settle into progressively deeper states of peace, concentration, and calm.

More penetrating insights into the underlying causes of suffering and the nature of any distorting illusions that give rise to suffering will develop. By stages, as you progress through this work, you will be ready to approach base level issues and practices of the way of liberation.

It is like the fire investigator's work. Once the fire is out, it becomes possible to see where the fire started and what caused the fire in the first place.

2.

The drawback to vanity is that any vain and conceited images active in a person's life cloud the mind and give rise to a whole host of thoughts and attitudes. These interior attitudes and vanities then drive the engines of anger, fear, excessive desire, and other stressful experiences.

Vain, puffed up, and inflamed aspects of self give rise to such thoughts as "I am really something special." "I am more attractive, or much smarter than most others." "My career and my possessions are all that really matter." "My wants and pleasures are more important than the needs of others." "Others are valuable only in so far as they can help me get what I want."

Vanity, conceit, arrogance, and fear cloud the mind and are among the driving forces which give rise to many of the desires people have.

Since many people feel they need certain achievements or possessions or some other status symbol to create a sense of self-worth, the desires to do what needs to be done to acquire these attributes can be quite intense. The same is true if someone threatens the props and crutches a person has based their identity and self-worth on. If a real threat to identity comes up, the desires for aggression or revenge can be quite pronounced. In fact the deeper the doubts one has about their self-worth, the more touchy they will be to even petty offenses. If such a person is ever in a situation where they feel they have been genuinely humiliated in their eyes and the eyes of others, the rage that surges can give rise to very violently aggressive urges and acts.

A way to extinguish the needs for false status and prestige needs to be found, especially for those whose sense of self-worth is particularly damaged.

The practice of cultivating humility is an important part of that search.

As the mind quiets, it will be more possible to explore how various forms of ignorance and illusion give rise to the general platform of self which, once formed, in turn gives rise to vanity and the excessive desires that arise from vanity, conceit, and arrogance.

3.

Fortunately, humility, like the willingness to try to love all beings, is a practice that anyone can learn if they are open to a few simple steps.

Humility is easy to understand and requires no advanced degrees or expensive weekend workshops to study. You do not need to go to some exclusive and expensive school to study humility or have some really lucky bounce of good fortune to be able to do so.

All you need is the willingness to be aware of any tendencies you have to try to puff yourself up or put others down and to look for any tendencies to judge others as being more or less valuable than one's self or others.

All you need is the willingness to remain teachable and supple.

All you need is the willingness to be small and unimportant in worldly terms.

All you need is the willingness to see, or to let other trusted people point out to you, the blind spots of selfish, vain behaviors or attitudes that mar your character and impede your chance of liberation.

The following suggestions are practical ways to cultivate humility. It is important to note that this is not some morbid process of self-flagellation or abasement. Rather these efforts are healthy ways to soften the force and blare of self and ego so a more natural, and more general, sense of self and a better chance for fulfillment can arise.

The benefit of this work is that it will help to noticeably enhance the delicacy and sensitivity of the interior state.

4.

Be very aware of the tone of speech you use when talking to others. Sadly, many overlook the tremendous value of the practice of Right Speech (another of the practices of the Eightfold Path of Gautama and Theravada Buddhism).

The simple fact is that really monitoring and refining the tone of voice you use when speaking to others (and the tone you use when referring to yourself) is enough to lead one to and through the threshold of enlightenment. This is because you will need to learn all the other lessons necessary for enlightenment to actually be able to practice Right Speech on a very consistent basis.

Are you speaking to others with patience, compassion, and respect, or with some tone of arrogance, condescension, self-righteous belief, smugness, or sarcastic dismissiveness?

The cultivation of humility will allow you to find a good, true voice and tone with which to address yourself and others. A big part of humility is to come back again and again to the precept that you are no less valuable and no more valuable than anyone else.

Do not wear any fancy fashions of dress or robes.

It is best to dress simply with solid colors and ordinary fabrics. Even if you are a vowed religious monastic it is best to dress in a manner more or less consistent with the fashions of your time but generally in a very simple version of your era's customary clothing. The distinctive garb of vowed religious people has value, but their habit can also be a significant trap if their special dress is too ornate or fancy. A common trap that arises for many, if they as a monk, nun, priest, abbot, bishop, roshi, shaman, or guru use special dress as one more prop in their covert drive to see themselves, and to have others consider them to be, a higher-caste person. It is not that the robes or special garments should never be used in the ministrations of rituals and sacraments. It is just that you need to be careful not to overdo it with special garments and to not become attached to the identity of being "the one who wears the priestly robes."

Do not wear jewelry of any kind unless it is some inexpensive religious symbol consistent with the tradition you have chosen. If you do wear such an adornment, it must be made of the simplest and least expensive material and design possible while still making this "possession" durable.

Do not wear any make-up, or seek to dye your hair.

Do not wear any mark of caste either openly upon your forehead or secretly in your inner perception of who you think you are.

With regard to possessions, make a conscious choice not to purchase anything that is showy or generally known to be a high-value status symbol. Make a conscious choice to be aware of the raft of emotions and urges that arise when you note that you actually are craving high-status possessions or achievements. Don't pretend that you are "beyond all that," if in fact you are not. We are all human and have our own version of the "bright shiny thing" that would enhance the rank others would ascribe to us in the social group we are part of. Find out from where such urges are arising and make very clear efforts to refrain from acting on such degrading drives.

Be very aware of the voice within that tends to separate people into different grades of worth and value. Be aware of the actual thoughts in your mind when you meet someone. Are you greeting them with respect, regardless of who they are, or is there a tone of noblesse oblige or some other officious tone of condescension in your voice or mind?

Do not compare yourself favorably or unfavorably with others for any reason or sense of competition but only as a guide to learn in what genuine ways you can cultivate virtue and learn from their positive or negative example.

If you have certain gifts and talents that you worked hard to cultivate, that is wonderful, but remember you did not cause the sun to shine that grew the food you ate that gave you the strength to do those things. It is also certain that you had the help of others, perhaps many others, who made your achievements possible, whether you are aware of this at present or not.

Neither did you make the talents in the womb that you were able to cultivate later in life.

Nor were you the weaver who wove your life from the flesh of your parents.

If others have certain gifts and values that you would dearly love to have, then let their good fortune be a cause for sympathetic joy. But remember, they did not give themselves their talents or even the ability to work hard to cultivate their talents. They also did not cause the sun to shine that grew the food that gave them the strength to do what they have done. Even the great geniuses of the world had the help of predecessors and many key helpers, whether they want to admit that or not. Neither did they weave their life from the loom of their mother's womb.

Should you be favored in the spiritual life with great visions, raptures, high ecclesiastical office, trances, or other powers or gifts or talents, then be grateful. But do not cling to them any more than you would cling to any pleasurable experience once it begins to fade and pass. The spiritual life is not about these phenomena, however wonderful or valuable such gifts and talents may be. Neither should anyone favored with such phenomena use them as the base of any kind of special status.

The real measure of a spiritual life well lived and worked is the increase one experiences in the naturalness and tenderness of the love they have to offer to others and their passive receptivity to be loved along with a willingness to serve those in greater need.

The spiritual life is the way of kindness, respect, charity, wisdom, humility, faith, and love. Anyone can choose these talents and gifts regardless of any other gifts, visions, or talents they do or do not have.

Do not listen to the flattery of others or take much note of any applause or acclaim you may receive, other than a simple acknowledgment of their compliments for whatever sincere offering you felt moved to make and were given the chance to make.

It is enough to know whether you are or are not in harmony with the deepest values you have chosen as the center of your life. Whether those values are God-centered or have some other tradition of compassionate wisdom as their center, it is enough to gauge to what degree you are being true to the highest standards of integrity you are aware of.

For those who do believe in God, or are willing to try to believe, it is enough to offer yourself as a willing servant to God and ask to be shown the true path to walk and to be given the strength to walk that path.

For those who do not believe in God, it is enough to be a skillful steward and witness of the tradition you favor and to be of service to those who ask for your help, and to be humble enough to ask for the help of others if you need to do so.

5.

If in the ordinary course of events and circumstances a leadership position is offered to you, or if others rightly urge you to seek one, then be available to such a position if it is consistent with the sacred path you feel called to walk. But do not clamor or connive to be at the head of the parade, or the monastery, or the great cause if such positions of leadership seem naturally to pass to others. There may be times when you need to compete for leadership positions if others who are clamoring for preeminence or power really are not competent or trustworthy stewards of church, business, enterprise, or nation. But whether you win such a competition or your best efforts come up short, do not be swept away in either case.

Those who are wise when they go to a feast "…go and sit at the lowest place." (Luke 14:7-11)

If the host wishes to move you to a higher place, then that will happen and you will be glad to be so entrusted. But if you seek to sit at the head of the table and the host has other plans as to who will sit there, then you may be quite embarrassed when you are asked to move.

Any who are wise know that leadership positions are a sacrifice and a distraction from other more subtle, calming, and profound efforts. The clamor and contention of doing anything with committees, coalitions, or crusades is a notable disruption of the beauty of learning to sit alone or with others in stillness, silence, and emptiness. The wise know it is best not to be caught up in the throng or din unless such is the path life presents to them. Those who seek the higher stages of the path know it is better to sit in a dark room or on a quiet hillside, or to chant the daily liturgy with a few good men and women.

Those who are given leadership positions that are rightly seen as being worthy and necessary do need to accept and embrace the work if this is the work that arises from the call they endeavor to be faithful to. But those who are passed by, or who miss out on positions of leadership are actually the lucky ones. This is the case assuming they are able to make good use of their luck by leading a quiet simple life of prayer and creativity off to the side of the madding crowd and the struggles of communities or empires.

6.

The desires to make some great scientific discovery or to write a widely-read book, or create some work of art of historic proportion, or to lead a great crusade of justice are more subtle but no less impeding forms of vanity and desire for power.

One only has to note how vicious and competitive many scientific, intellectual, religious, charitable, and artistic circles tend to be to note the suffering that arises from full-blown vanity active in these specialized arenas. Sadly, many caught up in these swirls of illusion do not see how much their vanity limits their ability to make full use of the insights and gifts they have been given.

Are you trying to build a monument to yourself that will endure after your death?

Are you contriving to be at the center of the stage to receive the accolades of the throng?

What is the point?

It is one thing if one is motivated by a childlike curiosity and wonder or some inner sense of personal call or mission to serve others in a particular way. But if all you are really doing is using spiritual, missionary, artistic, intellectual, commercial, or scientific efforts as a new arena in which to compete for rank and pre-eminence or the applause of the throng, then you are wasting valuable time.

If, on the other hand, you have been given some real insight and inspiration that allows you to make a genuine scientific, intellectual, spiritual, or artistic breakthrough, then it is important to relay that insight or creation to others. *It is also important to realize that key inspirations to your work came to you, not from you.*

It is important, however, in such cases, to have the humility to be a trustworthy steward of the message and not to be some clanging gong of vanity that uses the message as a prop of self and desire.

A willingness to serve rather than a hunger to lead is the hallmark of the humble steward or messenger.

Those who are wise know it is better to be a servant or a messenger in the kingdom of God (or the fields of the enlightened) than master of some pigsty or small brackish puddle. For trusted servants and messengers are often in close conversation with their master.

Another benefit is that a trusted servant is usually given the keys to the castle.

7.

Humility arises from the visceral realization and insight that you are no more valuable and no less valuable than anyone else.

No matter what you have done, or acquired, or achieved, you are no more valuable than you were at birth.

No matter what you have failed to do, no matter how poor or terrible some of the choices you may have made in your life may be, you are no less valuable than you were at birth.

Humility is an interior experience of softness and openness to experience both how valuable and how frail life is.

Humility is a way of being gentle within yourself and to others.

Humility is a willingness to do the unglamorous or dirty tasks when it is your turn to do a share of the unpleasant chores that are part of every household or community.

If it is your day to wash the toilet then do so with humility, gratitude, and dedication.

Humility is a willingness to face the unpleasant reality that you are not as good or moral a person as you pretend or claim to be. Humility is apparent when a person realizes in dispassionate self-appraisal how much they need to make fresh efforts with moral renewal and deeper faith.

Humility is a form of passive and docile openness to be led and instructed by God in the ways of life and morals, or if you prefer to phrase it in a different way, to the teachings of your sacred way if you have chosen a tradition that is not God-centered.

Humility arises as you begin to expand your horizons to see the vastness of life and that we as individuals are not the center of life, but rather one more small frail being trying to live as best we can on one small planet.

When you realize there are a hundred billion stars in our galaxy alone and that there are approximately one hundred billion galaxies with as many stars in the observable universe, it is possible to understand an old saying of sailors, "The sea is so vast and my boat is so small."

Over the past few centuries, as the general awareness developed of how vast the universe is and how small our planet and species are, many have felt this somehow diminishes the value of humanity into insignificance. Adjusting to being just threads in the fabric of life instead of the center of existence has caused many to go too far to the opposite extreme and feel that our lives are meaningless or worthless.

This is not true.

We are no less or more valuable than any other beings.

What very much seems to be the case is that our species and our planet seem not to be the center of existence, however shocking that may be to those still clinging to a medieval world view.

Given how small and frail we are as people and as a species, it is understandable that early peoples needed to feel they had a special relationship with the creator. This sense of a special relationship or covenant with a powerful warrior-God allowed small tribes to feel they could survive the wars and famines of their day because "God was on their side."

Tragically, this idea of a special relationship or covenant got tangled up with the instinctual drives for rank and control of larger territories and resources. Many tribes came to believe they were the most important tribes and that they could kill or enslave other tribes as part of their special destiny. In such cases, of which there have been many, the sense of special destiny or "covenanted relationship" of that tribe degenerated into drives to commit both overt wars of conquest as well as more covert forms of supremacy and domination.

The wars of aggression of Judaism, Christianity, and Islam over many, many centuries are classic examples of this tendency. The fact that all these cultures also have a very, very long history of slavery and exploitation, which continues in one form or another into the modern global economy, is another example of the destructive impact of mixing vanity, supremacy, and religion together.

This special sense of destiny and the accompanying covert or overt drives for supremacy have also had a tremendous influence on the formation of religious beliefs by distorting otherwise benevolent beliefs into violently intolerant theologies.

Many religious people came to believe that, rather than being the servants of all, their lot in life is to be the masters of all. Their teachings became the armaments of their drives for supremacy and the justification for their suppression of dissent and other challenges to their worldly power.

"You shall devour all the peoples that the Lord your God is giving over to you, showing them no pity…" (Deuteronomy 7:16)

"…you will rule over many nations, they will not rule over you." (Deuteronomy 15:6)

When one hears this comment from Revelation 12:5, "And she gave birth to a son, a male child, who is to rule all the nations with a rod of iron," it is hard to reconcile this with the comment, "the meek shall inherit the earth."

It would be difficult to overestimate how great an impact these drives for supremacy and dominance have had on the development of religion and how powerfully active such misguided views are even in the present day. All one has to do is look at the ongoing stupidity, corruption, and violence on the part of most of the factions in the conflicts in Jerusalem.

On a less visible scale, religious and monastic communities of all cultures, whether arch-conservative or very progressive communities, have more than their fair share of people who have learned to hide their secret drives for control and pre-eminence behind a false and sugary sense of humility.

Please be very careful not to fall into this trap, which is so easy to blunder into.

This would be a tragic waste.

Your chance for liberation is fully contingent upon the sincerity and skill of your efforts to be open to genuine humility.

8.

As a practical matter, when seeking to cultivate humility it will be helpful to gain a sense of how the silence of humility is different from the silence of a vain or secretly vain person.

The silence of the humble is far more quiet and pure.

The silence of the vain is just another blaring stream of noise and self-pouring from them.

The speech of the humble is a delight to hear.

The words of the vain, however correct they may be, still resemble a clanging gong or chest-thumping university don.

9.

Humility is never to be confused with cowardice. Courage is an essential attribute of the holy life, although the courageous have no need for medals or prizes for doing what needs to be done.

The consolations of faith and love are sufficient.

The consolations of faith and love are really sufficient.

These consolations more than make up for the letting go of vain desires, possessions, and prizes.

Trading humility for vanity is like receiving gold in exchange for mud-caked rocks.

10.

None of this is to imply that you should not have confidence in your value as a person, or take care with your appearance, or not feel satisfaction in the skills and crafts you have painstakingly learned to do well.

None of this is to imply that seeking reasonable levels of recognition and respect from one's peers is an unhealthy desire.

All that is being said is this:

> Watch all desires closely and carefully and see which desires are excessive and vain.

Watch closely any feelings, as they arise and pass, of self-aggrandizement or promotion, or being puffed up or inflated like some croaking bullfrog or some chest-thumping dragoon.

Which of your plans and desires are healthy and essential to well-being, and which are excessive or even destructive temptations you need to forego?

Try to understand that it is possible to waste years or decades or even your entire life chasing after goals and ambitions whose only real purpose is somehow to get you to a higher value in the pecking order of your chosen social grouping.

Watch all desires closely as though you were looking at them under a microscope.

When your concentration and insight develop to the point that it seems like you have traded in your ordinary microscope for an electron microscope, be glad. The precious gift of being able to explore in such minute detail the underlying causes of excessive desires and selfish agendas will help with the general efforts to diffuse such desires at their very source.

Insight and Illusion

Part 1

Foundations of the House

1.

In some respects all the work till now has been a long preparation for deeper searching.

While there is no automatic sequence, the cumulative efforts of the preceding practices to diminish anger, guilt, fear, doubt, excessive desire, vanity, and torpor will further quiet and clear the mind and heart. This work will make it possible to approach the remaining foundation issues that need to be addressed before the process of cultivating the best skills with concentration and pure interior silence can be completed.

What are the underlying causes that give rise to the conflicted emotions, thoughts, and excessive desires in the first place?

What are the underlying causes that give rise to the unending stream of distractions most experience in their efforts with meditation?

What illusions and delusions is one laboring under? How do the illusions and delusions one is laboring under catalyze the generation of conflicted emotions, thoughts, and excessive desires?

What insights need to be learned to find the best ways to diminish the underlying causes of stress and excessive desire at the source of their origination?

In other words, it is one thing to cut the weeds in the garden at the ground level. It is another matter to uproot them completely so they don't just keep growing back again and again and again. Actually, there is a less violent image that can be used instead of ripping roots out of the ground as though one were ripping traits out of the firmament of their psyche. This less violent image is to dissolve the roots of weeds below the surface by cultivating a deeper meditative calm and insight. It is like the roots simply wither and fade until they are no more.

2.

The Theravada Buddhists, who developed the teachings on enlightenment 2500 years ago, have made major contributions to world culture in the search for answers to these questions.

The problem is this: however worthy many of their detailed techniques and insights are, it is far from clear that some important aspects of their explanations of root causes are correct.

While the following comments are an over-simplification, they provide a useful overview of core analyses made by Theravada Buddhists of the underlying causes and springing mechanisms of conflicted emotions, thoughts, and excessive desires.

In the view of the teachers of this tradition, all suffering arises from some very basic but far-reaching causes. *Their first foundational insight into these underlying causes is that most people fail to realize, or are unwilling to accept, that all phenomena, and in particular all pleasures, are impermanent.*

Consciously and unconsciously most people remain caught in the illusion that some foundation for happiness, security, and identity that is supposed to be more or less permanent can be cobbled together.

Here is an important example:

If a person fails to realize that all pleasures are impermanent, this lack of understanding will give rise to a desire for a pleasurable experience to continue even when it is clear the time of that pleasure has passed. Such desires generate an attachment in a person's mind to an individual experience for it to remain as it once was. As the experience changes, tension is generated in the mind of the person who is trying to prevent the experience from changing. The problem is that the experience will, sooner or later, break apart, and fade away.

The stronger the attachment to keep things as they were, and the more the experience changes, then the greater the sense of tearing felt by the person laboring under the illusion that experiences could stay a certain way more or less indefinitely.

It would be best to let go, but this is exactly what many are unable to do.

For a commonly experienced example of suffering generated by a strongly forged attachment, imagine a romantic affair where the relationship began with great hopes but ends in disappointment and rupture. The one left behind, if they cannot accept the parting, may develop strong desires for things to continue as they were when love was fresh and new. The illusion that any set of constantly changing phenomena such as a love affair with another person can become a foundation for ongoing happiness and security is deemed to be the root cause of the attachment. The illusion that this one particular lover is somehow essential to this hoped for lasting foundation forms the specific clinging attachment. The illusion that it is possible to go back to the way things were, when the romance has clearly ended, is another springing mechanism that gives rise to further clinging. The harder a person tries to cling to the relationship the more forcefully the other will seek to break away. This creates a great deal of pulling and sense of tearing when the other person emphatically breaks away as often happens.

The fact there once were such intense and exciting pleasures in the romance, and such high hopes for the romance to be long lasting, generate a particularly strong attachment. When a person fails to realize that their hopes had been, at least in part, unrealistic the pain of those dashed hopes and the end of those pleasures will be all the more acute. This is especially true for those who did not have a strong sense of self-worth or contentment to begin with. The delusion that an exciting love affair would resolve deep-rooted issues of dissatisfaction with their life experience drives the intensity of the misguided grasping to find the right lover. The same illusions intensify the depth of the forged attachment should a lover be found who meets the designated criteria.

These same factors give rise to particularly strong emotional reactions if the highly-desired lover who was supposed to be the base of identity and completion then breaks off the relationship.

In all these ways illusion, delusion, and misguided expectations generate grasping and attachments which in turn generate very real experiences of heartache and suffering.

In most cases all that results is tears and heartache for a few weeks or months, yet even these levels of distress are truly painful for the one whose lover has left them. This can be especially true when the one who has left has departed to be with someone else.

There are times when the one who feels left behind may be so distraught they become very angry about what they feel is a betrayal of promises of everlasting love that were made to them. They may say things or lash out with real rage at the one they claim to still love.

In extreme cases, very aggressive desires may arise in the one who is left behind and they will begin to stalk and may even threaten or actually kill the one who has left. Who knows how many restraining orders are issued against former lovers who refuse to accept that the romance or marriage is over? Who knows how many people have been beaten or even killed by former lovers who are so enmeshed in a powerful web of delusion that they ignore the restraining order and go on the attack? Who knows how much suffering has been generated because some lovers have been unable to accept that the romance they had sought as a source of permanent happiness will in fact not be the foundation of their long-term happiness?

In such extreme cases of attachment one can see a vivid illustration of the general principle of how the failure to realize the impermanence of all phenomena, and the ensuing misguided desires to form a lasting foundation to identity and happiness, can lead to real suffering and a whole raft of painful emotions. This does not mean that many romances do not flower and last a very long time. What it does mean is that sooner or later there will be a parting. If a person is not fully aware and prepared for that parting when it comes, the attachments to what once was but which is no more can generate intense suffering.

Once a person does realize that all phenomena are impermanent and that what is impermanent can never provide the basis for lasting fulfillment much will have been learned. Once a person also sees how trying to prevent change in what is inexorably changing, they can begin to notice how often they do things of this sort in small and large matters. They can also mindfully observe the consequences of clinging attachments and resolve to shift their views, expectations, and decisions more in accord with life as it really is.

Another example of how the inability to see the impermanence of all phenomena gives rise to suffering can be seen when two people get married and are quite happy with each other, until one of the parties develops some highly self-destructive habits. Rather than accepting the reality that their romantic partner has begun to change in unexpected ways, the first person may make great efforts to resist the changes that are in fact beyond their control. Many romantic partners will cling to their former experience of their lover, when in fact their lover, and their experiences of their love, have changed in very deleterious ways. A person free from illusion and attachment will be better able to face and accept what has developed and implement an emotionally healthy decision to detach with love for as long as necessary. This scenario is another example of how anger, fear, and excessive desire can be traced back to a person's inability or unwillingness to understand that life conditions keep changing, often in unexpected ways. They can see more clearly what happens when their mind gives rise to the illusions that they can control certain changes in life conditions that in truth are beyond their control.

In another variation on this theme, imagine a romance does progress to marriage and the marriage endures and flourishes despite the inevitable challenges of any long-term relationship. But then the day comes when one of the marriage partners dies. This outcome, especially if the death is sudden and unexpected, will also give rise to great aching hungers for things to be as they once were. But everything is changing either slowly or quickly and death comes to all. If one is not well grounded in the reality of the impermanence of all phenomena and pleasures, their suffering at the loss of their loved ones will be greatly aggravated when loss finally comes. While almost everyone will experience a measure of grief at the death of a loved one, the depth of that agony and grief will be dependent upon how clearly one has seen and accepted that all phenonena is impermanent.

For a more prosaic but equally graphic example, imagine a local sports team has won a championship or several championships. Many people will find these victories to be very pleasurable and will want the team to keep on winning. But athletes age or are injured, or key players are traded and the team simply is no longer the same team it was. They start to lose more games than they win. Or in other cases the rival teams from other cities get a new coach or new players and they become the more dominant team. In the case where two cities view the others as arch-rivals, the excessive desire, anger, and fear about winning and losing to the hated rivals can generate surprising levels of stress in the minds of many people.

Look carefully at the passion generated by the competition for the World Cup in soccer.

How is it possible such passions are generated from a game about kicking a ball?

What is it that the spectators think they have won when their team has won?

What is it that the spectators think they have lost when their team loses the big game?

More drastic examples of the consequences that can arise when people fail to realize that all phenomena are impermanent can be seen in the rise and fall of dynasties, nations, and empires.

As a nation develops, some deluded person or clique gets invested in the illusion and delusion they can lead their nation in wars of conquest that will lead to the establishment of an enduring dynasty or empire. The delusion that worldly power might be permanent clouds the mind of many leaders and citizens of the powerful nation. Under the spell of this delusion, powerful desires, supremacist impulses, and nationalist vanities can be set in motion that will affect the lives of tens or even hundreds of millions of people.

This delusion and the excessive desires that arise from such delusions can then give rise to surging floods of rage towards anyone who threatens or is perceived to threaten such plans and illusions. Genuine mass hysteria can develop that a clique or a nation's enemies will somehow find a way to gain the upper hand. This is what happened in France during the Reign of Terror and in America during the McCarthy years and in China during the Cultural Revolution. Who can measure the suffering caused by those who foolishly thought they could build lasting empires or cling to illusions of worldly glory when inevitably empires enter into decline or violent upheaval?

From these and countless other examples one can begin to gain a greater understanding of how failing to realize that all phenomena are impermanent is a foundational illusion that gives rise to many excessive desires. From the extensive efforts to fulfill badly misguided desires myriad shades of anger, guilt, fear, vanity, and other conflicted emotions, thoughts, and desires can arise.

3.

It may take a while to fully see and comprehend how these dynamics unfold in various instances of everyday life.

One way is to consider how you imagine the attainment of certain major goals of romance, education, career, or finance are supposed to make you feel. *What do you imagine will be the impacts and gains to self-esteem and identity if indeed you attain the goals you seek?* How do you imagine you will feel about yourself if you get to certain heights in your career? How do you imagine others will regard you if you are able to attain certain important goals you have?

Who is it that you feel you will become if you get what you wish to have?

Now think back on how you felt when something happened that seriously threatened the attainment of a goal you decided was very important. Think also of how you felt during any situations where you had attained a desired goal, but then something happened that led to the unraveling or destruction of what you had achieved. Think also of those times when you simply did not find the deep satisfaction you had expected to find when you first chose a certain goal.

The more serious the threat to reaching an important goal or vain ambition, the more raw and visceral will be the emotions and actions taken to defend the chance of reaching the important goal or vain ambition.

None of this is to imply that one should not do everything they can to realize an important achievement or to protect that achievement from inappropriate encroachment by others. What is being said is that when you investigate the raw emotions that arise when something happens that threatens to undermine goals or achievements you have based your self-worth upon, you will see the magnitude and force of the forged attachments you have formed to the goal or identity prop being challenged. Once the power of attachments is seen, you can then gain a better sense of how much of an impact these attachments have in the larger field of the psyche. You will be better able to see how such clinging attachments and feelings of aversion constrict your inner life and generate one set of fierce impulses and distractions after another. You will be able to see how such attachments impede the cultivation of more supple and satisfying experiences.

A vivid example can be seen if a person acquires a high-status home and car and then loses their job or company to some treacherous competitor or unexpected set of circumstances. The emotions of anger and fear that arise as they try to hang on to their favored position and possessions may be quite intense. When one actually loses the fancy home and other possessions and actually becomes quite poor, the loss of prestige and the hardships that follow can literally eviscerate their sense of self-worth and identity. Naturally anyone would be distressed at such a reversal of fortune, but the more one tries to cling to the status symbols and the identity they tried to forge from those status symbols, the deeper will be the suffering at the loss. Instead of just being fully present to work with the situation that has developed, they will be beset by a whole slew of emotions and harsh judgments of self and others.

Another good example is the very real pain many politicians feel after being defeated in an election by someone they really despise. Another example would be if a top college athlete experiences an injury that means they will never make it to the major leagues, or if a big-time golfer misses the game-winning putt, or a high profile scientist loses a race to make an important discovery to a competitor team.

In the raw reactions to the kinds of changes to status and identity that really alter a person's life dramatically for the worse, one can see the depth of attachment people have forged to the props and crutches upon which they built their identity. When the props of identity are ripped from beneath a person, it becomes possible to see in general how shaky had been the foundations upon which a person contrived to build their house of self.

Hopefully no such dramatic changes will happen in your life. But if they do, know that you can make good use of these experiences and changes. You can see how deeply embedded and how transitory are the props and crutches most of us try to cobble together as the foundations of our self, ego, and identity. You can see what images of self you are trying to create or are clinging to. A diagnosis of a terminal illness and the news you have only a few months to live is one such dramatic example. The betrayal of adultery by a marriage partner is another, especially if you had no idea such an affair was happening and then suddenly find out.

In the most extreme cases where there is not enough food or water for everyone who is present, you will see how all semblance and pretense of morality and civilized behavior will tend to be stripped away. It is in such dire circumstances where there is not enough room for everybody in the life boat, or not enough food to keep your family from literally starving to death, when the full power of the instincts for survival and the attachment to life will be laid bare. It is under such extreme pressure, real or perceived, that a person or a nation will discover who exactly they are. This is what happened to Germany in the 1930s and 1940s and Russia in the 1920s.

While such situations can also call forth the best and most selfless acts on the part of some people, anyone who has ever lived through a truly desperate situation will know what is being alluded to in these observations. It is these raw passions or potentialities of passion that lay as dormant possibilities within most of us until conditions develop that activate them. *The veneer of our civility and the flimsiness of moral resolve are among the most important illusions to see clearly.*

Fewer insights will do more to support the cultivation of humility and the search for a more viable and robust foundation of morality than this one.

Becoming more aware of how you might react in extreme situations will provide a vivid illustration of the full power of instinct, desire, and the puffed-up aspects of self and ego. You can backtrack to the more ordinary circumstances of your life with a renewed sense of urgency to extinguish grasping, attachment, and aversion. You can see more clearly what goals you have, what you hope those goals will do for you. You can see more clearly what are the status symbols and props of identity, self-worth, and vanity you feel you need and may be clinging to.

In the midst of the ordinary changes of everyday life there will be less energy wasted trying to resist change.

As skill and sobering insight develop, you will be all the more clear and stronger.

You will be far better prepared to respond to and endure any major upheavals in your personal life or in the society in which you live. It will be far more possible to see through any illusory or magical thinking that may be active on your part or others and let go of what you need to let go of. You will be far more able to retain a sense of clarity and focus on what is essential in any given situation.

From the cultivation of such insights and skills equanimity will arise.

The quality of equanimity, that is to say not being swept away by either good fortune or bad, is a primary factor leading to enlightenment as taught by most traditions of Buddhism.

4.

None of this is to imply that people should not make every effort to achieve a favorable outcome to any important situation or to provide for their family in times of great privation.

None of this is to imply that people should not make every effort to find healthy viable relationships or to find reasonable levels of security and stability in this life.

What is being said is that it is helpful to be fully aware of any illusions you have about how certain attainments or achievements are supposed to make you feel should you be able to realize such goals. The same can be said for having realistic expectations as to how long lasting any attainments or achievements might reasonably be, if indeed you reach the goals you had set.

Another admonition is that you be fully aware of any illusions where you fool yourself and others into thinking you are further along the path of realization than you actually are.

Look closely and notice the anger, fear, excessive desire, and suffering that arise if you find yourself struggling badly to attain intensely-desired goals. Take the time to *notice how often you claim some thing, or person, or place to be "yours" or "mine" and how you feel when something claimed as "yours" or "mine" is taken from you.* Take the time to notice also any dissatisfaction that arises when you do attain a certain goal or acquire a certain possession only to find the experience does not satisfy anywhere near as much as you thought it would.

What is also being said is to use every inch of your skills with awareness and compassion towards yourself and others when you notice you are moving through your life like a hungry ghost or when you try to hold time in your hand by squeezing your fist more tightly.

5.

So far much of the Theravadin analysis that certain illusions are the underlying causes that give rise to suffering and misguided desires seem to be reasonable enough. But what may possibly be fundamental errors arise as these teachers deduce further conclusions from their core insight about the impermanence of all created phenomena.

They feel that since all phenomena will someday break apart and be completely dispersed *then there is no enduring center to anything.* Most importantly they assert this is also true of people.

As a consequence of these deductions, teachers of this tradition have concluded there is no such thing as an eternal self or soul. Even more importantly, they have also concluded that since there is no actual lasting center to anything there also is no such thing as God as the eternal self or soul of the universe. For them a belief in an eternal God is essentially a projection by the individual of the wish for an eternal self. In their view, letting go of beliefs in an eternal God is part of the process of letting go of a belief in an eternal self.

The realization and acceptance of these cardinal insights is deemed to be central to the traditional Theravadin method of meditation instruction if a student wishes to attain enlightenment.

In the Theravadin view, before a person can really let go of attachments to various external phenomena or internal hindrance they need to be willing to let go of the idea of a permanent self or soul.

The process begins by endeavoring to see the impermanence of all created phenomena. These mindful observations make it possible to see that the self too is a temporary aggregation of attributes, each of which arises from different causes. In simpler terms: when a person is young they may think "I am young." When a person is old they may then think "I am old." If a person thinks "I am a beautiful person" and then they are badly disfigured in an accident they think "I am now a disfigured person." *Since the experience of what constitutes the self is constantly changing as the conditions of life change, it follows the self is a transitory phenomenon that has no intrinsic or enduring reality.* As the self is a transitory phenomenon with no lasting center it follows, in their view, that it makes sense to let go of any rigid definition of what the self is or is not.

The more attached a person becomes to the delusion that this construction they call their self can somehow be a fixed and permanent reality the more that person will suffer. They will launch one plan after another to accumulate possessions and experiences that are supposed to be the lasting foundations of their identity and happiness but which never can be so. The more fixated one becomes that any pleasure or prize will somehow be lasting, the more that person lives like a hungry ghost that can never be satisfied. In their view, the endless string of mildly or sharply dissatisfying experiences in the present life becomes an endless cycle of births and deaths in countless future lives. The hungry ghost drifts in abject misery from lifetime to lifetime until they finally awaken and see through and then extinguish all operative illusions and delusions.

It is not that one no longer labors to attain the essentials of life or to build a house or monastery to live in that is as solid as possible. It is not that each individual who believes in this way is supposed to become some colorless automaton. It is more that this doctrine is an especially vivid way to emphasize the need to let go of all self-centered fixations. This general teaching is offered by Buddhist teachers as a way to help people refrain from the counter-productive attachments which arise to people, places, and things when a person fundamentally misunderstands where and how to find satisfaction.

This doctrine of the emptiness of self is offered to help people see that their sense of identity or self-image is built upon a foundation of props and crutches that are constantly changing. The older one gets, the more possible to see this perception clearly. The general idea is that while one tries to build the most stable life they can for themselves and those they love, it is important to stop chasing after pleasures or prizes as *though the experience of such possessions can do more for you than they actually can.* It is also important to recognize that change is inevitable yet often comes in unexpected ways. By knowing this one can more flexibly accept and work with change as it comes.

In the view of the teachers of the Theravada tradition, accepting this perspective helps a person become free.

They feel that letting go of the idea of God as the permanent self or soul of the universe is part of the process of letting go of the idea of a permanent self or soul. They feel such clear thinking allows a person to stop chasing mirages and experience life for what it is.

In their view, letting go of a sense of permanent self or soul is like being in a country where a selfish and incompetent king that has managed to cling to power for decades finally dies. Everyone, except the sycophants of the king, breathes a sigh of real relief. The leading citizens of the realm then resolve to manage the affairs of state with a wide degree of involvement from the citizens without relying on any one dominant personality.

Whether you agree or disagree with the elemental conclusion of Theravada doctrines is not so important at this juncture. What is important is that the meditation techniques of mindfulness, insight, and concentration they have developed to peer into the foundations of the self, and the illusory assumptions of self, and the causes of excessive desire, are very valuable.

These techniques enable people at least to correctly gauge the magnitude and complexity of the general problem faced by those who seek to diminish the underlying causes of excessive desire and suffering, and the distractions that arise during meditation.

6.

The problem is that these teachings that assert there is no permanent self or soul and no such thing as God are disturbing concepts for many. The same is true for the doctrines that assert that all experiences lead to suffering and that all talk of life after death is a complete fiction can also be quite disturbing to those raised in God-centered cultures.

But whether these teachings are bleak and disturbing is also not so important.

What is important is this:

"Are the teachings that there is no permanent self or

soul and no such thing as God as the central and eternal life of the universe true teachings or are they mistaken illusions?"

"Is the image of a God as infinite and eternal merely the ultimate anthropomorphic projection of the deluded wishes of the self and ego to endure forever?"

Before considering these questions let us return for a while to the original questions raised in the opening of this chapter.

What are the underlying causes that give rise to the conflicted emotions, thoughts, and excessive desires and the unending string of distractions that arise in most people's practice of meditation?

What are the best ways to diminish the underlying causes of stress and agitation and all these distractions at depth?

For those really struggling in their life to find a clear direction and some genuine relief from harsh emotional or physical suffering these are not academic questions. Neither are such foundational questions merely academic pursuits for those who are committed to finding fresh ways to diminish the underlying causes that lead to violent oppression, injustice, and harsh poverty in societies around the world.

How can we learn to teach the ways of liberation and wisdom so that more people can more readily understand how to diminish the root causes of suffering in their lives and therefore better support the transformation of the societies in which they live?

Let us continue these sustained reflections.

7.

Catholic, Greek and Russian Orthodox cultures, as well as others view the root causes of all suffering and excessive desire very differently than do the Theravada Buddhists and other atheist cultures.

These equally venerable, beautiful, and at times equally dysfunctional cultures view the source of all suffering to be the sinful desires and behaviors of Adam and Eve and their root disobedience to God's clear commandments. Most teachers in these traditions view this primordial fall from grace as the motive force which has created the suffering, disordered passions, and death we experience in this life. In this view of original sin it is the individual's willful rejection of the Church's moral code as revealed in the Bible and the rejection of the supreme divinity of Jesus Christ that is the source of all personal and societal troubles. The disobedient self gives rise to ever escalating cycles of sin and disordered passions that can never be satisfied and which are the destroyer of people, nations, and churches.

In their view the sacraments of the church, one's adherence to their church's moral teachings, and the mystical reconciliation with Jesus by grace and faith are the only way to diffuse the underlying causes of excessive desire and suffering.

Foundational to this view is that each person has a soul that lives on forever after death and that entrance into eternal life in heaven is the ultimate end of suffering.

Needless to say these teachings about the underlying causes of excessive desires and suffering, and immortal destiny of individuals are very different from the teachings of the Theravada Buddhists.

It is also worth noting that the venerable cultures of Muslim Sufis, Jains, and Hindus also generally agree the righteous self does survive after death, in a state of immortal love and peace and that God very definitely does exist. They feel it is the primary duty of adult life to conform to God's ways as the best way to build stable families and societies and to gain the great rewards of immortal life, rapture, and love.

In short, after death we find a pleasure and fulfillment that never fades or comes to an end.

But whether these teachings are beautiful and consoling is not so important.

What is important is this:

> "Are the teachings of the immortality of the soul and the perfection of God's grace and love true?"

Which is it?

Are the soul, and the immortality of the soul, and God nothing more than illusions?

Or, are the teachings that there is no soul, and no immortality of the soul, and no God the illusions that one must see through?

Or is it possible that there are only parts of these answers that are true, and other parts that need to be set aside?

How can one come to understand the true causes of excessive desire and suffering so one can diminish these underlying causes and come to know the perfection of peace and liberation?

What is the truth of the matter?

Is there any way to decide which of these two very different visions of life is true?

8.

These are not unimportant questions, and indeed they were questions well known to Gautama and the early generations of his followers.

He and they tended to dismiss such questions as being distractions that wasted valuable time that could be better spent in far more beneficial pursuits. This approach of dismissing such jungles and swamps of speculative thought deserves serious consideration.

However, successive generations of Theravadin teachers, from ancient times till now, seem to want to have it both ways. They want to claim that thinking about such questions is a serious distraction to the simpler practices they feel are proven means to attain enlightenment. Yet teachers of this school then go on to definitively state that these questions have been resolved. In their view there simply is no such thing as an immortal soul and no such thing as an eternal God. Furthermore, in magazines and books and dharma talks all over the world, Buddhist teachers assert that reincarnation is an irrefutable fact of life. They make this assertion irrespective of the fact that there is little in the way of convincing scientific proof to support this claim. *If reincarnation is as central to life as photosynthesis or genetics then where is the proof and mechanisms? While the work to gather empirical evidence in support of reincarnation by such researchers as Dr. Ian Stevenson is interesting, it is far from conclusive.*

The seriousness of these assertions is compounded by their view that unless a person renounces a belief in the immortality of the soul they cannot attain Nirvana. This is no small matter. They continue: if a person does not renounce these beliefs, and does not attain Nirvana in this life, they are inexorably condemned to be born into a new life perhaps in a much lower life form. They teach that until one renounces a belief in the immortality of the soul and in God they will be born and grow, suffer, age, and die again and again until they do renounce these beliefs and attain Nirvana.

Many Christians are just as emphatic about what is at stake in their vision of life and truth and are perhaps even more rigidly resistant to any discussion about their important dogmas.

In the view of conservative and arch-conservative Christians if a person does not accept Jesus Christ as their Lord and Savior and conform to the moral codes of their Church then that person *will live forever in excruciating pain in hell with no hope of appeal.* Many Muslims and Hindus have their own equally dire version of ultimate rewards and punishments in this life and after death. No doubt many countless religions of the smaller indigenous cultures of the world also espouse similarly dire warnings or threats.

Many modern people, especially those with sophisticated scientific backgrounds, may simply shake their heads and smile at the competing visions of monks with their threats about what happens after death. Many others who make a passing study of religion or spirituality are disgusted at what they feel are such perverse teachings. Consequently they either just walk away or may even come to believe that religion is in general quite a toxic poison which needs to be extirpated from human culture.

But many who turn to meditation for needed relief may not be able to shrug the matter off so lightly. Given essential intuitions they have gained about the beauty of liberation or the unity of all life, they perceive that something of inestimable value can be gained by Right Understanding (Another of the practices of the Eight-Fold path of Gautama and Theravada Buddhism).

Diametrically opposed teachings and threats such as the ones cited above can cause a great deal of anguish for those who have high levels of anxiety and are struggling to find real relief.

After all in most monasteries or convents and many churches a visitor or a member will hear such foundational teachings and threats repeated again and again. This is true even in those settings that are genuinely positive and hospitable in other ways.

"…whoever does not believe is condemned already." (John 3:18)

Those who have high hopes for what is possible for individuals and societies who are able to gain Right Understanding may undergo similar angst as they try to discover which is the true path that leads to wisdom and richness of experience.

Understandably, one who either cannot understand or cannot accept some of the foundational teachings of the culture they are involved with may well feel they are missing something of vital importance. Even worse, they may become terrified about their fate after death. Even if a person is living a fundamentally virtuous life, they hear again and again the dire warnings and threats of what happens to those who do not accept core doctrines. Given the nature of those threats it is easy to imagine *the degree of conflict that may develop in the mind of some people.*

They may feel in good conscience a visceral need to set aside certain seminal teachings but are still very much afraid of the consequences of doing so or what they might miss by not submitting to established doctrines.

While most societies have progressed beyond the burning of dissidents, the threats of intense suffering after death for those who do not believe correctly are still read in many church services and retreat centers around the world. Tragically incidents of violent attack and even murder by fanatics still occur in the early 21st century against those who refuse to accept their harsh beliefs.

As this book was being finished a Christian cabinet minister in Pakistan was assassinated by fanatics for questioning the heresy laws in that society.

Even if a person is not influenced by such violent warnings and threats, the issue of not being able to accept core dogmas can still be quite troubling.

The prolonged suffering many feel in their lives is oppressive enough that they have a compelling need to make sure they do not miss any essential teaching that would allow them to find the healing relief they seek.

Given the depth of their need it is all the more important for such people to see if they can understand and accept what are presented as the foundational explanations of the path of liberation they are studying.

After all, it is the foundational teachings of a religion that seek to explain the root causes of suffering and the means to diminish suffering that all other teachings are built upon.

Adherence by the believer to these foundational teachings is taught *as being instrumental in diminishing suffering at depth and gaining the great offered reward.*

These are not small matters.

Many find themselves in a real bind as they attempt to convince themselves to believe things they really don't. They attempt to do this to see if those beliefs might be the missing pieces they need to awaken vividly felt experiences of illumination and thereby find some real relief from suffering. Others who have found a greater degree of personal stability, but who seek enhanced ways to diminish the suffering of others also feel a passionate need to discern more fully the truth of liberation.

But many find that the difficulty of choosing between different religions is only part of the challenge. What do you do when none of the foundational explanations from any religion really make as much sense as they are supposed to? What do you do when you go looking for essential truths and do not find what you are looking for however profound and valuable many aspects of the teachings and cultures you encounter may be?

Where do you go when there is nowhere that really feels to be quite right?

How can we find new ways to help those in need of deep healing for whom existing teachings and remedies are not effective?

How can we discern a sufficient measure of true belief and practice that is more clearly understood and therefore more fully embraced by wider sectors of the population?

What teachings are needed to help more people more readily come to know a satisfying richness of experience, peace, and freedom?

Insight and Illusion

Part II

Above the Tree Line

9.

If you feel you do know the answer as to whether you do or do not have an eternal soul, it makes sense to commit in deeper faith to the answer you feel is true. It makes sense to follow the teachings and the teachers of the path you have found with ever greater fidelity, diligence, and sincerity.

10.

If you are not certain, but are inclined to believe in one answer or another to this important question, then it makes sense to make, at least, the next level of commitment you can to the path and community of believers you feel most closely drawn to.

Even if you still feel a sincere need to hold back from a full commitment by saying, "Yes, these are the truths I have been seeking," *you can still take some additional risks to have at least a little more faith in the teachings you are exploring.* You can utilize this extra measure of faith as an additional way to explore the truth and efficacy of the tradition you are studying. *You can then see what experiences arise from these additional risks with faith and immersion, and see where the path leads from there.*

Stronger commitments of faith in the teachings you have embraced before you actually have all the tangible evidence and insight needed to support those commitments continue to be necessary risks of any spiritual path. But the gradual stages of the simple path will help you discern what incremental, or quantum, risks with faith you may be willing to commit to. As experience and insight continue to accrue from each stage of practice, you will have more personal evidence to consider as you contemplate additional commitments of faith.

An important benefit of the simple path is that there is no need, and no coercion, to take drastic leaps of faith. Small steps with faith, made over time in a good general direction that feels right to you, will be sufficient.

In simpler terms, you can stumble before you walk, and you can walk before you run.

Put another way, you can dip your toes in the water, then walk out up to your knees, and then to your chest, before you decide whether you are willing to dive all the way in. If you walk out to your chest and find the water too cold, or the waves too big, you can return to shore and seek another part of the beach or another beach altogether to re-enter the water. Or, if you do feel assured, you can dive in and swim out to the hauntingly beautiful islands of mystery and unconditional faith off the coast.

For those favoring an atheist way such as the Theravada Buddhist path of meditation, you can proceed with a greater level of trust with the teachers of your chosen tradition whose personal example you feel is most credible. You can see if the answers they give, and the example they set, feel good and true according to the best standards of integrity and honesty you apply to such discernment. You can then gauge the impact to your personal experience in both meditation and your active life as you follow the guidance these folks have presented, and make further decisions from those evaluations.

For those who favor beliefs centered in God's divine love and mercy as their means to seek illumination, you can pursue the same incremental efforts of holding more innocent trust and faith in the teachers and the teachings of your chosen tradition. But to these efforts you can add one more. You can be still and silent and use your inner voice to begin to open a dialogue with God. You can do this as though you were talking to some very kind person sitting right next to you. You can do this in the language and context of whichever religious tradition you feel most drawn to.

"O God I open my heart and mind to your guidance and living presence."

"Help me to know the true nature of my life and the true nature your life."

"Help me to know in what ways our lives are joined and to feel more deeply the communion of our shared life."

"Help me to feel more deeply the blessings of this communion and to join my life to yours more completely."

"Help me to understand what happens to the believer when their body dies."

You can ask in humble silence and then wait in humble silence to see, over time, what answers and experiences arise within you. A truly humble and docile submission to the emergence of the living presence of God's grace and love is a good way to allow deeper experiences of the divine assistance to develop in your life. From this deeper experience you can explore whether you feel you could make stronger commitments to the path of divine love and grace. Don't be surprised if there are no sudden answers to your supplications. *It probably will take longer than you want it to,* but you can trust that real answers will come to genuinely sincere and open-minded supplications.

If you continue to fumble as you seek to decide between the atheist way or a God-centered approach to the great awakening, see which seems to be most true to you as you gaze into a young child's eyes or upon the dazzling night sky over mountains.

As long as your search is accompanied by mature commitments to virtue and a steadfast effort to offer your love to all who live, you will find your way.

11.

If you really cannot decide whether you do or do not have an eternal soul, or whether God exists, or which religion is the right one to follow, that is all right too.

Let the confusion and uncertainty simply be confusing and uncertain.

It is enough to look closely at the actual experience of confusion with a careful mindful attentiveness. Without judgment, look closely to see how this confusion feels in the mind, heart, and body.

It is enough to greet the experience of confusion with a wider and more generous sense of patience, affirmation, and acceptance.

It is enough to honor the doubts and questions you have.

It is enough to remember you can make the conscious choice to infuse your experience of confusion with compassion for yourself and for all who walk a pilgrim's path without being sure exactly where they are heading.

You can set aside those teachings and questions you do not understand or which you feel really may not be true. You can always gain benefit by making more sincere and refined efforts with those practices you do understand and can freely embrace with your whole heart.

There is a secret to this method that is well worth the knowing.

By committing a higher degree of consistency of effort and sincerity to the simplest of practices than most ordinarily would, you can reach astounding heights of understanding and experience.

The experiences, intuitions, and insight that develop by this gradual approach will always open a way forward to the next level of peace and understanding available to you.

This is the simple path.

12.

As the stress and agitation in your life are diminished by diligent application of the earlier practices, *your skills with awareness, concentration, and insight will continue to develop.*

As the mind calms and clears, your experience of self will continue to simplify.

And, as you continue to simplify your experience of self, your mind will further calm and clear.

You will be more able to touch the core tensions of self which remain and more effectively learn how to unclench these tensions. With each degree of relaxation and "letting go" you will be able to see more clearly into the foundations of self. The insights that will arise from this ongoing investigation will help you, in turn, to see how to further simplify the experience of self and to observe more clearly the moment you are in.

There will be fewer and fewer distractions that arise which hijack the mind off into one unplanned diversion after another.

If your primary practice is centered on concentration practice, you will more clearly see any and all potential distractions for the empty and impermanent conditioned phenomena they are and dismiss them without prejudice. You can simply and very consciously return your focus to the sensations of the breath at the top of the upper lip and the opening to the nostrils without being swept away in any of the distractions that arise:

It will be as if you are a skilled soccer goalie who can see where the shooter is aiming by the way they prepare to kick and then gets into position to deflect the shot that is coming.

As you become adept with concentration practice you will be able to sustain your focus on the subtle changes of the sensations of the breath for longer and longer periods of time. You will be able to see how many micromoments there are in the changing sensations of a single cycle of the breath, or in a single repetition of the sacred word or phrase you have chosen. It will be easier to sustain your concentrated awareness on each nook and cranny of the sensations of the inhale, the top of the inhale, the halting pause before the beginning of the exhale, the long slope of the exhale, and the long hiatus at the bottom of the exhale before the new breath begins.

It will become clearer that it is the transition at the top of the inhale before the exhale has really begun that is one of the places a distraction is most likely to be able to slip through and steal your mind away. You will see more clearly the fine nuances of the long slope of the exhale and then the long hiatus at the bottom of the exhale before the next inhale. The long slope of the exhale and the hiatus before the next inhale are other common points in the cycle of the breath when some distraction is most able to slip through and hijack your mind. In particular, at the bottom of the exhale, and the long hiatus before the next inhale begins, there are very few sensations to observe. At these points, look more closely and carefully. You will see there are some barely perceptible sensations of air faintly swirling at the top of the upper lip and opening to the nostrils. You can also be aware of the very fine sensations of the flesh in the upper lip and the opening to the nostrils. These observations will allow you to sustain your concentrated focus on this narrowly drawn point until the more tangible sensations develop in the new inhale.

It will be possible to be extra vigilant as pinholes develop in the seam of your concentration, pinholes which are large enough to allow distractions to slip through and carry the mind off in some semi-conscious lapse. It will be more and more possible to seal those pinholes before they develop into the full breach of unplanned distraction.

It will be more possible to sustain a steadier awareness on your single point of focus. *Still, concentration will probably not be so established that there are no distractions.*

The basic questions of the nature of the self and the emptiness of self as the Buddhists say, or the surrender of the self and will to God as the Christians, Muslims, Hindus and others say, continue to be important questions to study. However much work you may have done to greatly slow the mind and the number of distractions, more insight into these general issues will be needed to attain very high degrees of interior silence and single point concentration. *Before proceeding with those reflections in section 15 below, please note the following additional comments.*

13.

If on the other hand you are working more with insight practice as your primary practice rather than the more narrowly drawn efforts to attain single point concentration, *this is another good way to process confusion over what to believe.* To engage insight practice you can sit down and begin a meditation session without any preconceived agenda other than to begin with a simple focus on the breath. You can make the conscious choice to observe in increasingly finer detail and then investigate any bodily sensation, emotion, thought, or image which arises into prominence in the mind. Perhaps you will wish to maintain your awareness on the breath as a centerpiece to your efforts while also being aware of a shifting range of these other sensations, feelings, or thoughts. Perhaps you will withdraw your focus on the breath and give your full attention to whatever sensations, feelings, or thoughts that arise; the choice is up to you.

If theistic images or feelings arise of God, or the Sacred Heart of Jesus, or Allah, or Tara, or some other genuinely sincere devotional image or experience, then simply observe and fully honor such experiences as they arise. Observe carefully as pious images or devout sentiments come to fullness, then peak, and then begin to break apart, and finally pass from the center stage of your awareness. When they pass you can simply let them pass and remain alert and aware as new moments and experiences continue to unfold, or as similar images and feelings return anew.

If non-theistic inclinations or images arise that lead you to think there is no lasting center to your life or self or to any dharma, then you can observe such images, thoughts, and feelings as they arise and pass.

If experiences of real confusion and repetitive word loops keep circling about the various questions and choices of faith, then simply observe without attachment or aversion these phenomena as they arise and pass.

As long as you do not make the mistake of thinking it is all right to allow immoral or unwholesome images to take root in your mind, you can gaze at the river of images and thoughts that arise and pass through the screens and fields of your interior life. As each experience arises, spreads, peaks, and passes there are a few simple questions to ask:

> Is this experience satisfying or unsatisfying, or is it neutral?
>
> Does this experience lead to the cessation or the proliferation of suffering?
>
> What do I need to do now to diminish the suffering or pain that can be diminished?

This practice of insight and investigation, without judgment or attachment, of whatever images, beliefs, sensations, or thoughts arise, is another excellent way to cultivate the insights that lead to equanimity and freedom.

You can simply watch the shifting fields of the interior experiences the same way the keeper of a lighthouse watches the ceaselessly changing cycle of seasons and weather as they generate changes to the color, form, and texture of the harbor and sky.

This level of clear, alert, and detached awareness will refine consciousness in ways that are similar to advanced stages of concentration. This is because well-developed insight meditation is essentially another variation of concentration practice. It is just that with insight practice it is the act of sustained watching that is the single point of intention even though the focus of what is being watched continues to shift from one point to another. But, and this is important, in a well- developed practice of insight meditation it is always a conscious choice of what to focus upon, not some semi-conscious drifting.

As you peer deeply into the true nature of individual phenomena, with sufficient detachment and alert clarity, you will gain insights into the general nature of all phenomena. These insights will give rise to the wisdom needed to understand how to proceed to extinguish the underlying causes of stress, illusion, delusion, and suffering.

Still it is unlikely that insight will be sufficient enough for true equanimity, which is the prelude to full enlightenment, to arise. Something else still seems to be needed. This should not be too surprising.

Finding true and effective insight into the foundational questions of the nature of the self and soul *is just as important in insight meditation as it is with concentration practice.*

14.

Longer cycles of sitting and walking meditation are an essential part of this "something else" that is needed for the higher stages of practice to develop. This is true irrespective of whether you favor concentration or insight as your primary practice.

Longer retreats of seven to ten days with a dedicated focus on your chosen form of practice will allow for notable incremental increases in practice ability and understanding. As the time away from daily responsibilities is increased, the body and mind will slow down more than is the case when one is juggling daily practice with multiple home and work concerns of everyday life. It is simple: your mind will continue to simplify and further decompress. This comment is made with the assumption that the practical details of your preparations for longer retreats have been well planned.

Still, it is not likely that these longer retreats will automatically become times of effortless peace, although that might happen. Rather, these retreats may be surprisingly difficult at times with little in the way of ease or consolation. After all, in some ways longer retreats are a very specialized setting where the full force of interior conflicts and doubts are given a wide space to emerge from the basement of the mind into personal consciousness. It is for this reason that a skillful guide who really is open to understanding and honoring your particular journey is an important support to an extended retreat.

Still, it continues to be true. Longer periods of time for meditation practice over a number of days, when one is more or less free from everyday concerns, will allow for higher degrees of concentration and insight to develop. What you can count on is that, sooner or later, and for many it may be later rather than sooner, very pure experiences of peace and calm will develop. While the actual experiences of those who favor concentration work as their primary practice may be different in nuance from those who favor insight practice, the benefits of either will be well worth the efforts of the journey.

As you become quite proficient, longer retreats of two to four weeks will probably be needed before the best skills with concentration and the full ripeness of insight can be attained.

It is simple. To reach the higher stages of clarity and peace, significant periods of time away from daily responsibilities will be needed. This is especially true for people who have generally high-strung temperaments and a tendency towards emotional intensity in their life.

As always, it is helpful not to be too daunted by such commit-ments of time. As you progress with simplifying your life and strengthening your regular daily practice, the ability to consider more challenging retreats, and commitments to faith, will develop somewhat naturally. Still a strong sense of determination and prac-tical preparation will be needed to actually take the time for such retreats. See if you can get whatever projects you are working on to a state where they are either completed or at least can be set neatly on "the shelf" until you return. The same holds true for any personal concerns or practical problems that need to be addressed. There is little point in going on an extended retreat if you will be constantly preoccupied by matters that really needed your atten-tion before you left for the retreat.

As a final caution, if you have never done at least one or two seven to ten day retreats it would generally be unwise to attempt a longer retreat of a month or more until you have completed intermediate level retreats.

15.

Still, even after sustained and noble efforts, for many, it is the foundational questions about the nature of the self and the pos-sible reality of the immortal soul that remain to be answered.

Can one really attain the higher stages of meditation without mak-ing a decision they can commit to in pure faith as to whether they do or do not have an eternal soul and whether God does or does not exist?

This is a useful question and if you feel you have found a true answer then peace to you and all the best for you have found your path to walk. But if you are genuinely uncertain as to how to answer this question that is all right as well. The following specific efforts will help continue to quiet and clear the mind even if you really are not sure what the answer to this question might be.

At this point you may wish to re-read the chapter on "Humility" to review the foundations of your efforts to cultivate a mature practice of humility, and then come back to this section. For a solid foundation with humility practice is an essential part of the work to diminish any glaring manifestations of vain and selfish attitudes and behaviors. This work continues with the efforts to then diminish any of the ordinary levels of vain and selfish attitudes which remain active in your life. Having progressed with care through these first two stages of work, the efforts to simplify the more subtle and submerged plans, schemes, and agendas of self can proceed.

16.

You can proceed by looking carefully at both unconfident as well as overconfident images of self that arise as you go through different moods and situations. Be aware when any sense of low self-esteem, or any sense of needing to be very impressive, or any thoughts that you are very impressive arise, peak, and pass away. What is important is to begin to realize you no longer need to identify with any of these feelings and images of self, or think of them as anything other than the chimera they are.

Patiently and compassionately, over time, you can learn to diffuse any unconfident and overconfident images of self by no longer agreeing or accepting that the descriptions they present are accurate descriptions of who you are. This is a good bit of intermediary work. *This will allow for a good measure of the necessary simplification of the sense and experience.* The result will be a healthier, but somewhat more general, sense of being "you." It will be all right to be just another decent person who is one among many. It will be all right to be just one of countless life forms in the countless realms of existence. This by itself will be a real relief for many who have struggled their whole life with either feelings of low self-esteem or with impulses towards grandiosity. This work is another stage in an incremental process of simplifying the sense and force of self.

Every stage of the simplification of self will reduce the number and the force of distractions which arise during meditation and in the active hours of everyday life.

Every stage of the simplification of self will also allow you to derive a clearer sense of the true nature of self and of the larger realm of being in which we all live.

Every stage of the simplification of self will allow you to let go at deeper levels of the subtle and submerged plans, schemes, and agendas of self.

17.

The next stage of this work is more subtle.

You can begin to observe all the baseline descriptors you generally use to describe who you are.

Good examples of these baseline descriptors are one's gender, age, race, body image, talents, character flaws, character assets, nationality, religion, sexual orientation, your achievements and your failures. Most are unaware that these descriptors are constantly playing in the background of conscious experience. These descriptors form the foundations of the sense of who we think ourselves to be, and the sense of who we think others see us as being.

All of these descriptors add to the thickness of the bundle of associations, drives, and memories we vaguely refer to as self and ego. It is the constant playing of this shifting bundle of mental formations that creates the general continuity of identity. It is this bundle of memories and definitions that causes us to wake up every morning and still be more or less the same person we were yesterday. It is this bundle of mental formations constantly being replayed at a sub-conscious level that creates the general sense of self we experience as "us" in the dreams we dream during the night.

Patiently and compassionately you can begin to let go of these various descriptors, strands, and layers of the bundle of self by realizing that none of them are really "you."

None of this is to imply that one should no longer refer to those descriptors which are accurate when it is appropriate to do so in everyday life. After all, no matter how advanced you become with meditation we all still have the same date of birth and parents and general description of our body and personal history to date.

What is being said is to begin to realize that who and what you are at a very fundamental level is not defined by your gender, age, race, body image, nationality or creed, or any other of the descriptors you commonly use in everyday life. *This realization will help further reduce the thick sheaf and massive neural bundles we refer to as "I" or "me" and allow your personal experience of self to further simplify.*

You can begin to notice how often you define who you are, or who you are afraid you are becoming, by commenting to "yourself" within your interior dialogue, or in conversation with others. This process of self-definition comes about by making various statements such as the following:

> I am this. I am that. I am not this. I am not that. I have succeeded at this. I have failed at that. I own this. I do not own that. Others have more than I do. Others have less than I do.

> I am old. I am young. I once was young, I now am old. I am attractive. I am not attractive. I am not as valuable as this one. I am more valuable than that one. I am who I am because I have the job or the home that I have.

> The way others treat me must be the way that I am. I like blue. I do not like pink. I believe in Buddha or Allah. I believe in Jesus and Mary. I believe in God. I do not

believe in God. I believe in sex, drugs, and rock and roll. I am a liberal. I am a conservative. I have done well. I have done poorly. I am a person with bad health. I am a person with good health. I am the guy who never gets what he wants. I am the guy who always gets what he wants. I am the gal who never gets the man she wants. I am the gal who made a good decision in marriage. I never get it right in relationships. I am the divorced one. I am a pathetic loser. I am incredibly successful. I am stronger than my competitors. I am weaker than my competitors.

Once again, some of these descriptors will continue to be accurate and necessary in some ways as you function in everyday life. It is just that in the final analysis these descriptors are incidental to the true nature of who and what "you" are.

You can also begin to notice how often you refer to something or someone as "mine" or "my this…" or "my that…" Your mind will continue to calm and clear as you learn how to see and then let go of the attachments you have formed in your mind to anything you have labeled as "mine" which is not actually essential to your life. A simpler way to say this is: seeing and then letting go of even the subtle forms of controlling and possessive thinking and behavior will also greatly aid the process of simplifying the tone and sense of self.

What is also important is that as the sense of self is steadily simplified so too the experience of consciousness becomes steadily refined.

This simplification of the sense of self is needed to be able to cultivate the best skills you can with concentration and insight. Letting go of all attachments to that which is not essential and to all illusions will allow you to observe your life, and all of life, more clearly and simply.

These comments are made with the assumption that one has engaged the practices of confession, repentance, and atonement in ways that wash away the stain of sin or, as the Buddhists say,

defilements. For harmful deeds done to others which are not con-
fessed, repented, and atoned for will define and circumscribe who
you are, and who you can become. As noted earlier, confessing
and atoning for any gross or subtle anti-social acts or thoughts is
essential to making any meaningful progress with meditation and
the search for liberation.

This diffusion and "letting go" of all of the images and descriptors of self is supported by the general work of humility and the
work of cultivating ever more refined insights into the nature of
your interior life. The hard images of self and ego will noticeably
soften and fade. Whether you follow the Theravadin or the Christian way, or some other faith tradition, the experience of self will
become more general, open, and translucent.

As you do this work, the storm and cloud of what we vaguely
call the self and ego will further subside. With this willingness to
cultivate a soft, quiet, humble, and passive tone to your interior
experience you will be "...*thinning the sense of me.*"[7]

Wisdom and more penetrating insights will continue to accrue to
your benefit.

18.

It is not that self and ego are intrinsically bad. Quite the contrary,
both are needed for everyday life and especially for the more difficult aspects of the struggle for survival. Neither are the instincts
and the impulses, volitions, and thoughts that arise from them
intrinsically bad.

It is just that even moderate and reasonably well-adjusted levels
of these interior forces are able to generate a great deal of tension
and agitation in the mind. Until these faculties and tendencies

7   Stephen Snyder and Tina Rasmussen, *Practicing the
    Jhanas.* Boston: Shambala Publications, 2009, p. 36.

of the mind are quieted, real peace will continue to be elusive. It will not really be possible to "let go" completely or to cultivate high grade skills with equanimity.

The Buddhists view the outcome of this final letting go differently than do Christians and others who follow God-centered traditions. Teachers of these different traditions also approach the training needed to get to this level of peace and insight in different ways.

But for any sincere person seeking meaningful transformation in their life the core work is much the same.

By working to diminish anger, guilt, fear, excessive desire, vanity, torpor, and illusion the number as well as the force of the impulses arising in the mind will be lessened. They are lessened to the point that our personal consciousness is no longer swept away by this or that impulse, doubt, or emotional surge. Once the mind becomes more settled and cleared it is possible to gaze upon the base activity of the mind. It is possible to simply observe as the contracted core of the mind continues to generate various impulses, sensations, feelings, and thoughts. The experiences of peace and clarity that a person has come to know by this point of the journey are enough to generate intuitions that even more refined states of peace and calm are possible. The beauty of this prospect is appealing enough that it simply makes sense to allow the remaining dynamic tensions of the mind to unclench. This "letting go" will further diminish the number and the force of the impulses and distractions generated by the mind.

Having spent many years mindfully observing the consequences of acting on impulses and desires, important lessons have been learned. Some of those lessons are that even the positive experiences which arise from successfully gratifying the impulses and desires of the mind are nowhere near as satisfying as the prospects of perfect peace and sacred beauty. These lessons are made even clearer by the frustrating experiences that arise when one has not been able to gratify the impulses and desires which were deemed to be important. The very negative and painful consequences which arose from those times when a person was able to gratify misguided or openly immoral impulses are even more convincing proof of the need to try a very different way to attain peace and fulfillment.

As these various lessons and insights are gained, usually at a fairly high price, the vestigial impulses and desires of the mind lose their allure and magnetic appeal. As one is no longer mesmerized by the allure of the impulses, there is little if any effort expended to act on those impulses. With very little value placed on these impulses and with little if any effort made to act on these impulses they further fade away until they are dissolved.

In simple terms, when you stop putting any wood on the fire, it goes out.

It is like you are gazing upon a very special interior sea where the surface of that sea is constantly trying to gather together and give shape to a formed face and head. After a while you realize it is you who are providing the force that drives this sea to constantly try to form this face, or sense of identity, fashioned from the gathered waters of the surface. The strings of words, images, thoughts, memories, and desires are the various building blocks of the base effort to build a foundation for this formed face of identity and sense of self. It is not that a clear and healthy sense of identity and self are not needed for everyday life, for in fact they are. What is being said is to learn how in silent meditation to allow the forces beneath the surface of this interior sea to simply "unclench." Learn how to bring to rest the constant fashioning process of words, images, thoughts, desires, and identity. Take the time to see how clear and radiant this interior sea can become when you are able to allow the waters of this sea to be very, very calm and placid. Take the time to learn how these experiences of deep rest and calm will help you be more clear, alert, and creative in the course of everyday life as well.

Let the heart and mind be truly silent.

It probably is best not to pay too much attention to anyone who says this work is easy or quick. The same is true for anyone who says it is not possible.

While the celibate person walks a different path to the river than do those who are sexually active, at some point the paths converge. Those who are sexually active will need to have periods of their life where they can diffuse the sexual impulses as part of the effort to diffuse all impulses and volitions. Those who have family and householder responsibilities will need to have fulfilled their responsibilities to the point that they can find extended time for intensive practice or retreat away from everyday life. In truth it is much harder for the householder to extricate themselves from the busy-ness of life for long enough periods of time for real practice to be possible. But, with care and patience such conditions can be arranged in one's life, at least over time. Having said this, it is not as though the life of a celibate person is some easy path. While they should, generally, be able to lead a far more simple life, the work needed to attain a viable celibacy is a significant effort. As noted earlier, both ways of life have their very real challenges.

Do all desires ever truly go away? No. The need for food, water, and sleep, and other basics continues as long as we live. It is just that when the needs have become very simple it is possible to meet them in ways that do not consume a great deal of energy. When these needs are met they become quiescent for a while. *The satiation and quiescence of essential needs and desires, combined with the diffusion of all non-essential desires through discipline and insight will be enough.* The activity in even the base strata of the mind is reduced to the minimal levels needed to sustain life, breathing, and posture during meditation.

When the mind and body have become this quiet, it becomes possible to experience the true nature of all phenomena and being. Different people will come to different conclusions about what is signified by such sublime experiences. But for any sincere person seeking meaningful transformation in their life the core paths they take will have much in common.

They will find there may be plenty of times when it seems like the efforts and sacrifices they have made to persevere on this journey are more or less a fool's errand. The work needed to quiet the conflicted thoughts, excessive desires, and nagging doubts will often seem to be too hard. Many may feel again and again that they have come to a dead end. It may seem that while others may be able to complete the journey they may feel they personally just do not have the strength or skills that are needed. The vagueness and confusing language of much of mystical commentary and the troubles in whatever spiritual or monastic tribe they have joined will appear, at times, to be too much to bear.

But then, through the next level of commitment to those simple practices they do understand and can accept, the way to the next deeper level of peace and understanding will open for them. Thus refreshed they will be able to keep going. From each new threshold of peace and understanding the next, and then the one after that, will come into view.

19.

As virtue, humility, detachment, and insight further refine, the force and experience of self will further simplify. As the experience of self is further simplified, it will be possible to diminish all non-essential desires.

Your experiences of peace and clarity will deepen significantly. *It will finally be possible to cultivate the best skills with concentration that you reasonably can.*

The very refined experiences of peace, concentration, and insight that develop will give rise to marked enhancements to your faculties of intuition, faith, reason, and perception. These enhancements to your abilities with intuition, faith, reason, and perception are one of the great benefits of all the tedious and painstaking work of contemplative study.

As you emerge from these very refined states, you will be able to work more skillfully with any questions you feel continue to be relevant.

The question at hand may be what to do about some hard choices in everyday life. The issue under consideration may be some baffling challenge about how to diminish the chronic physical or emotional pain someone is suffering from. The unanswered question may be whether each person has a soul or not, or some other elemental theological quandary. The unsolved puzzle may be some daunting challenge of theoretical physics or universal cosmology.

With regard to the central question of this final chapter, as the mind clears, it will be as if you have dismantled a house. Finally, you will be able to see the foundation of the house, the house of self, and the ground beneath the foundations of this house of self, more clearly.

Perhaps you will come to believe there is no soul or lasting permanent center to this house or to any other phenomena.

Perhaps you will see the ground beneath the house of self is luminous with the light of the soul and that the soul is somehow a channel through which you can receive God's infinite love and through which you can offer your love and devotion.

Perhaps you will come to believe that there is no individual soul, but that the universe of which you are a part is a single, vast, multidimensional soul and living being.

Perhaps you will come to believe something different from any of these three perspectives.

You may ultimately find a way to choose between, or to reconcile, different views of religion or philosophy that previously you could not. Or, you may never really be able to come to any final conclusion about some of the important questions you started with. In either case, the exceptional peace and clarity of very refined states of silent inner freedom, and very tender experiences of compassion, will render remaining unanswered questions less and less relevant.

This is a good path. This is a true path. This is a simple path.

20.

At any point along the way, if you find you are favoring a path to liberation where there is no belief in God or soul or immortal life, then commit without reservation or hesitancy to faith in these beliefs. This comment is made with the assumption that you remain committed to the highest personal standards of moral living and personal integrity. With these qualifications in place, clear your mind of any vestigial beliefs in a permanent self, soul, or God. Let go of any attachments to beliefs in an ongoing life-after-death in either material or immaterial form. Let go of any hazy notions of the presence of God in the vast panoramas of mountain scenery or the dazzling night sky seen from a hillside desert cave. Experience the emptiness of self and the emptiness of a universe devoid of any notion of God or prime mover. Let go of all the plans, schemes, and agendas of self and all thoughts of all other people and creatures.

Steadily, the sense of self will continue to be simpler and more general. As the experience of self is simplified, the number of distractions in the mind during meditation will steadily diminish. With the body completely still, and all desires and acts of volition extinguished, it will then be possible to let go of even the efforts to support wholesome impulses and to restrain impulses that are anti-social. *Since there are no actions, desires, or mental formations being generated there are no consequences (or karma) generated. It is only these unique circumstances that allow a person to forego even the last bedrock of duality, which is the duality of good and evil.* This will further simplify the centers of will and volition. This is the final letting go of volition and self. The deepest sense of interior quiet and the most refined states of concentration will arise. Even the sense of there being one who knows, and the sense of any object known to the one who knows, will fade and be no more.

This is a very advanced level of concentration known in the Theravada tradition as the eighth Jhana practice, also called the stage of "neither perception nor non-perception."

With concentration practice all the impulses and factors of the mind are gathered into a single moral, or morally neutral, focal point. This is the middle stage of the path. Proceeding to allow even this single point of reference, or aspect of self, to soften and fade is the passage that leads to the higher stages of the Jhana practices. These higher Jhana states, which are emphasized by some traditions of Theravada practice more than in others, are one way to develop the ability to gain the insights needed for final liberation.

21.

On the other hand, if at some point of your journey you feel called to favor a path to liberation that affirms the reality of the soul and the infinity of God as the foundation of all existence then commit to unconditional faith in these beliefs. This comment is also made with the assumption that you remain committed to the highest personal standards of moral living and personal integrity.

Begin your meditations with a conscious choice to make a silent offering of your love to the God of heaven and earth or some similar act of conscious choice. Open your heart and mind to receive the intimate gift of the divine assistance in return. Turn your thoughts to the place where your love for God meets God's love for you. See if you can touch the light of God with the light of your heart and then let these orbs of light and sentiment converge.

If you find the mind wandering off in distracted thought, make the conscious choice to draw your attention back to offering your love to God, or just a simple gazing at God. Engage the discipline of setting aside all other thoughts of all earthly prizes or creatures. Open your heart and mind and soul to the revelation of the living presence of divine life and love in the very depths of your soul.

Humbly and passively consent without reservation of any kind to a more free circulation of grace through every level of your being.

Draw your awareness to the realization that the God of heaven and all the raptures of heaven are literally present in the depths of your heart and being as they are in the depths of all who live. Consent to the mystery of the experience of being touched directly and joined in the center of your soul in intimate and delicate communion with God almighty. Feel the joining that is the mutual holding and gazing where you and God are suspended in each other's love the way the sun and the earth are suspended in the fields of each other's gravity.

Let go of anything and everything that impedes the fruition of this most tender love so that this embrace can deepen into final union. Surrender in complete and natural assurance that you will live forever embraced by God in perfect love and grace.

In the Carmelite tradition as described by St. Teresa of Avila, this is what is known as the Prayer of Quiet and the Prayer of Union. The Hesychast monks of the Greek and Russian Orthodox tradition call this "pure prayer" or "the prayer of the heart." No doubt there are many equivalent terms from other traditions as well. It is not that one takes, at this point, the prospect of their salvation for granted, or becomes complacent in their faith or diligence. Rather one has simply reached the fruition of faith in divine love that they know they can trust fully in this love regardless of what happens with the painful trials of their life.

22.

But, if you continue not to be sure what is the true path to follow that is all right as well.

Spend a few weeks or months, or longer if you need to, with each of the credible choices you are evaluating. Go back and forth again and again like some pained and confused teenager between the choices you are considering, assuming that any choice you are considering is centered in the practice of unconditional love for all beings.

Keep searching for more practical and skillful ways to meet the genuine challenges of your life.

Honor the questions you have and the answers you have found so far.

Be true to that which is most true within you.

Honor the sacrifices you need to make to remain true to that which is most important within you.

Be open, really open, to insight and revelation.

Never be unwilling to admit if and when you have lost your way. Never be unwilling to admit if you realize that some of what you formerly believed, or may even have taught to others, is not quite as true as you once thought it was. Never be unwilling to embrace teachings which you once rejected, but which you now feel are worthy of real commitment.

For any who are sincerely willing to follow the search for truth, wherever that truth may lead, will find their way.

This is a good faith. This is a true faith. This is a simple faith.

Epilogue

To reach a place where the heart and mind are very quiet and clear for sustained periods of time during meditation is to reach the middle stages of the journey. This point in the journey may even be two-thirds of the way towards the final destination. While there is much more to be learned about concentration, insight, and affirmation practice, this threshold of experience is a good place to rest a while. Here you can be refreshed by the peace, clarity, and freedom you have come to know.

It is as if you have reached a place above the treeline where the vistas are wide and very, very beautiful. One can also see the path that leads on to the summit even if the summit remains shrouded in clouds.

Still there is time now to pause and to enjoy the peace and sacred beauty that was sought for so long. There is time to be refreshed by the cool mountain air and renew one's strength for the ascent of the higher stages of the path.

As you do the work needed to reach this place, be as patient as you can be, but work as diligently as you reasonably can. Extraordinary efforts that only a few are capable of are not needed.

It is enough to realize how much can be attained by a steady and sincere cultivation of very basic practices over the years and decades of your life.

If someday you have the privilege of working with others who are just beginning, or who are at some earlier stage of the path, be sure to honor the doubts and struggles of their life as well. Be as patient as you can as you learn more about their life. In any attempts to be supportive of others, it is important to remember to speak in a very natural way. Before offering any suggestions or guidance please always ask if the other person is interested in hearing your comments or would rather simply value being listened to or if they prefer just to be left alone.

Please also remember this: other than the search for your own awakening, there is no greater or more solemn responsibility and privilege than to teach the way of awakening to others.

Be as careful as you can that what you teach is, at the very least, free from serious error.

Whenever you are not sure about something, please qualify your comments appropriately. Comments such as "I think this is true but I am not sure," or "This perspective helped me, but I am not sure it will also work for you," will help convey you are still reflecting on the subject at hand but that what you are saying is nevertheless worth their serious consideration. Suggesting a person seek the counsel of one or two other mature people on any important question is another good way to encourage people not to become dependent on any one personality, including yours. This suggestion will help people with one of the primary goals of spiritual mentoring, which is to find the right balance between seeking the counsel of others and thinking for themselves after careful investigation.

Never teach anything to others with powerful conviction unless you genuinely believe what you are saying is true.

The insight that permeates this work is very simple. There are far greater resources within and around us than most of us are able to perceive most of the time. There are more creative ways to make contact with these resources and to draw upon the life of these resources that are yet to be discovered which will help diminish the suffering of even harsh trials.

We need to find ever more creative ways to search for and draw upon these resources.

May all wounds be healed.

May all truths be known.

May the purity of perfect peace and love be known to all who seek.

May all who fall, no matter how far they fall, be given numberless chances to change their life and find the healing they need.

Amen.